# The Hedgerow Circus

Written by Ruth Thomson
Illustrated by Jolyne Knox

PUBLISHED BY THE READER'S DIGEST ASSOCIATION LIMITED

It was Midsummer's Eve.
All seemed quiet in the hedgerow,
but there was magic in the air.

The ants scurried here and there.

The beetles skittered and scuttled.

The bees buzzed back and forth.

The butterflies flitted and fluttered.

The hedgehogs sniffed
and snuffled.

The birds cheeped
and twittered.

At last everything was ready.
The stage was set.
The feast was laid.

The hedgerow circus was about to begin.
"Roll up! Roll up!" called the ringmaster, dressed smartly in a spotted coat.
Everybody gathered around the stage.
"Let the show begin!"

The grasshoppers were first.
The smallest one leaped
on to the middle of the stage.
"Aah," said everyone.
The middle one leaped
almost to the far edge.
"Ooh," said everyone.

The largest grasshopper of all jumped all the way over the stage and landed on the other side.

"Wow," said everyone, clapping loudly.

"Who's next?" asked the harvest mouse.

"It's my turn," said the spider,
twirling round and round
on his thread, lowering himself
at great speed.
"Watch this!"
This way and that he swung,
up and down, round and round,
making a web before everyone's
very eyes.
The audience cheered.

The spider sat proudly
in the middle of his web
and took a bow.
"Who's next?" asked the harvest
mouse.

"Are we next?"
shouted the hedgehogs.

"No," said the ringmaster,
"It's time for the tug-of-war."
The caterpillars twined themselves
round the bindweed stalk
and got ready to pull.
"Wait," called the ringmaster,

"We've forgotten the line."
The snail had an idea.
She slowly crept her way forward
leaving a thin slimy line behind
her, right between the two teams.

"Right," said the blackbird,
who was acting as referee,
"Are you ready to begin?
On your marks, get set, go!"

The caterpillars pulled
with all their might.
First one way
and then the other.
Who was going to win?

It seemed an even match,
but all of a sudden,
the peacock caterpillar lost
his grip.
The hairy caterpillars
were tugged over the line
and fell together into a heap.
The audience clapped wildly.

"Who's next?" asked the harvest mouse.

"Is it our turn?" the hedgehogs asked again.

"Not yet," said the ringmaster firmly. "Now it's time for the butterfly dance." The butterflies, who had been quietly feeding on the flowers, rose silently up above the hedgerow.

Higher and higher they flew,
darting and fluttering
in the warm, still air.
Their colours glowed
in the evening sunshine.
"How beautiful," chorused
everyone.

"Who's next?" asked the
harvest mouse.
"You're next," said the ringmaster.
The harvest mouse turned pale,
but hurried over
to the nearest stalk
and climbed up.

"Look at me," he cried,
nimbly jumping from one stalk
to another, using his tail
to help him.
Everybody watched open-mouthed.

"Us next?" asked the impatient hedgehogs.
The ringmaster shook his head.
"The shrews are going to do their trick next."
Two shrews came on to the stage and bowed to the audience.

"I'm going to hide," said one.
"And I'm going to find him," said the other.

The second shrew shut his eyes ...

whilst the first one jumped
into the audience and crouched
behind a wren.
The shrew on the stage
opened his eyes.
First he sniffed the air...

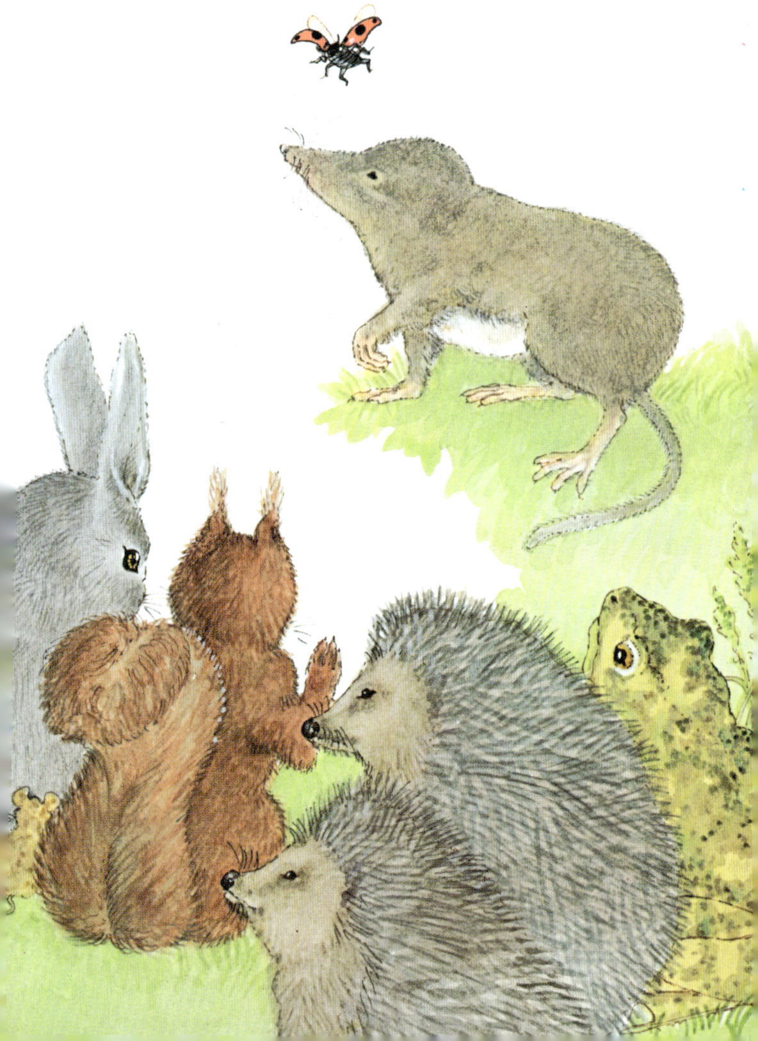

then he sniffed the ground
and walked towards the wren.
"There," he said, pointing
triumphantly, and up popped
the hidden shrew.

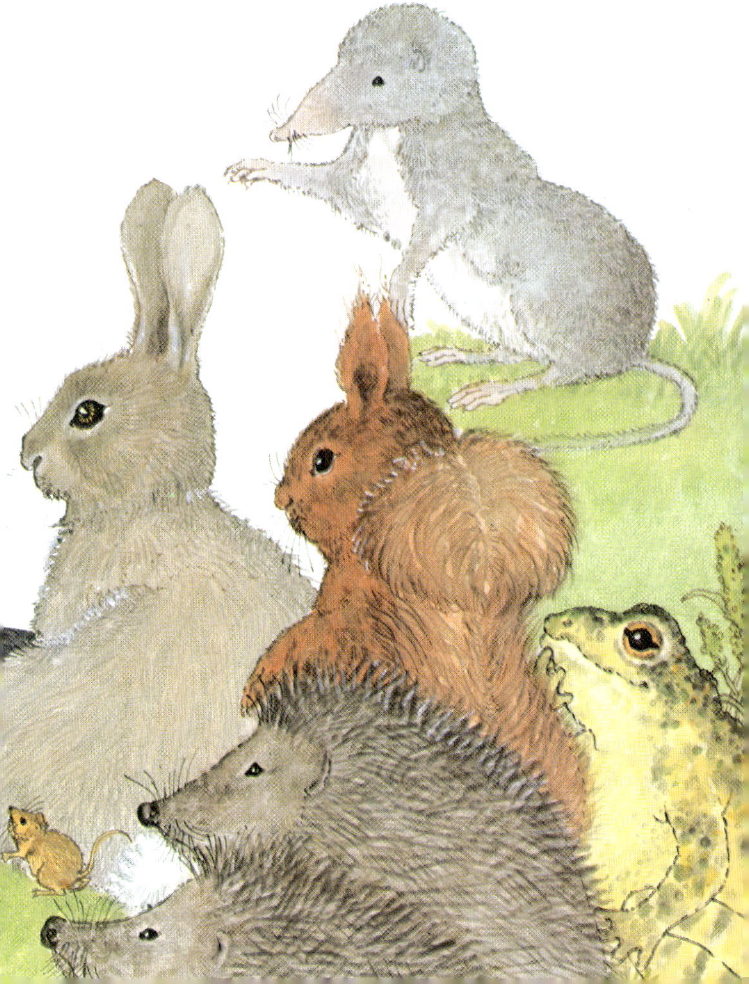

"And now," said the ringmaster,
"it's the hedgehogs' turn."
The audience waited eagerly.
But what was that?

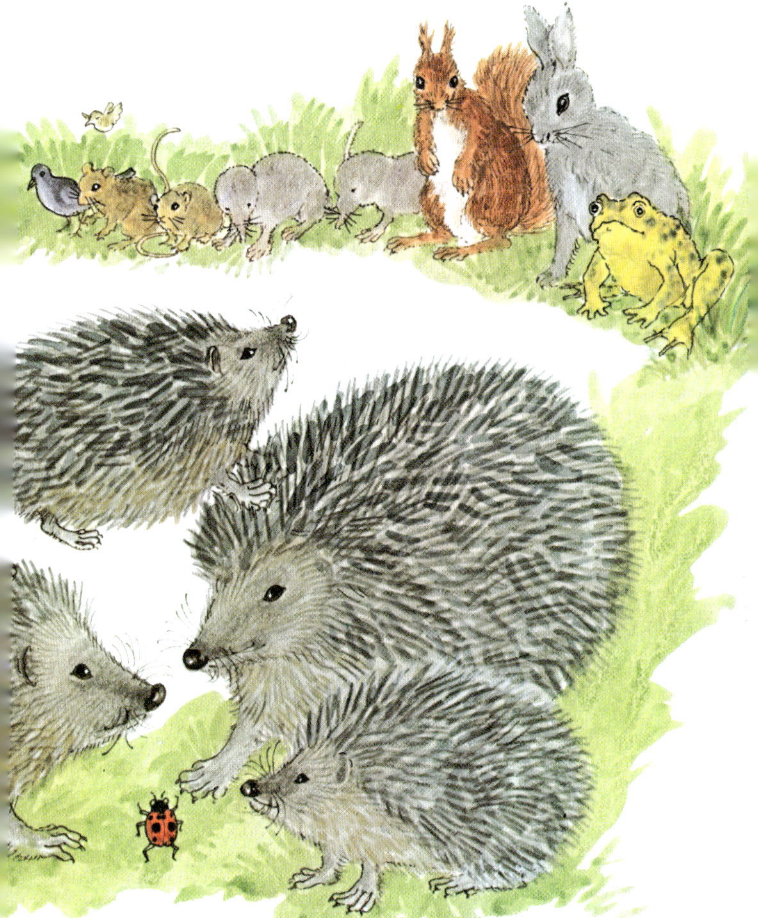

Clomp! Stomp! Clomp! Stomp!
Clomp! Stomp! Clomp! Stomp!
Noisy thuds came closer and closer.

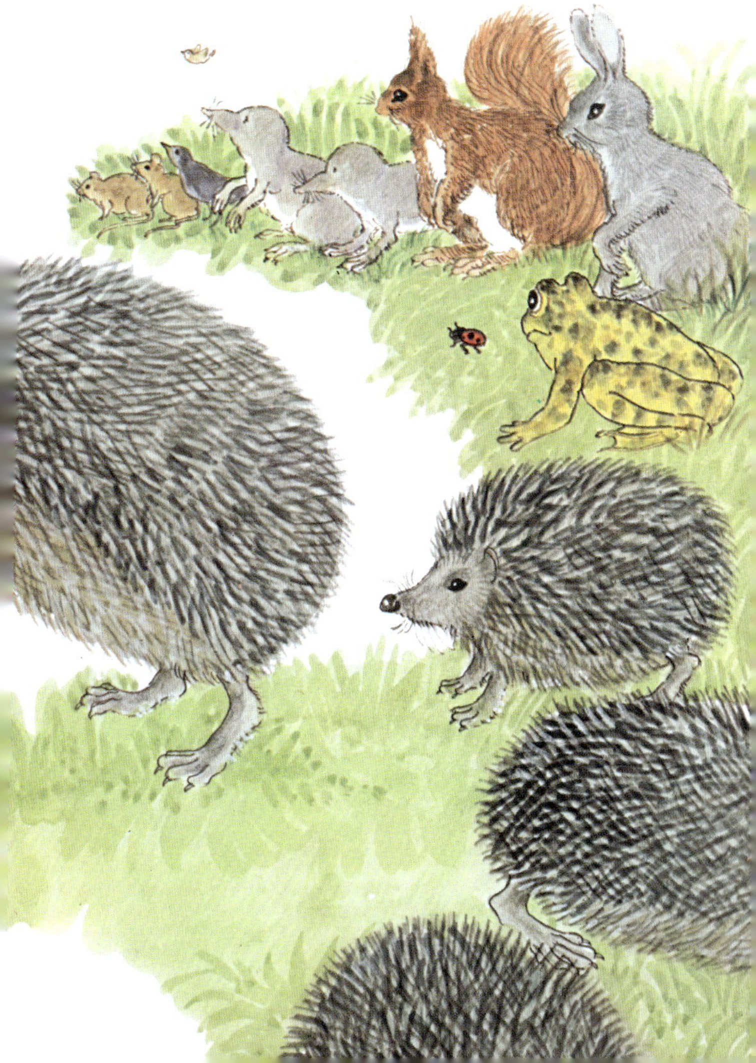

"Run!" shouted the ringmaster.
"Hide!" squealed the harvest mouse.
The animals scattered.

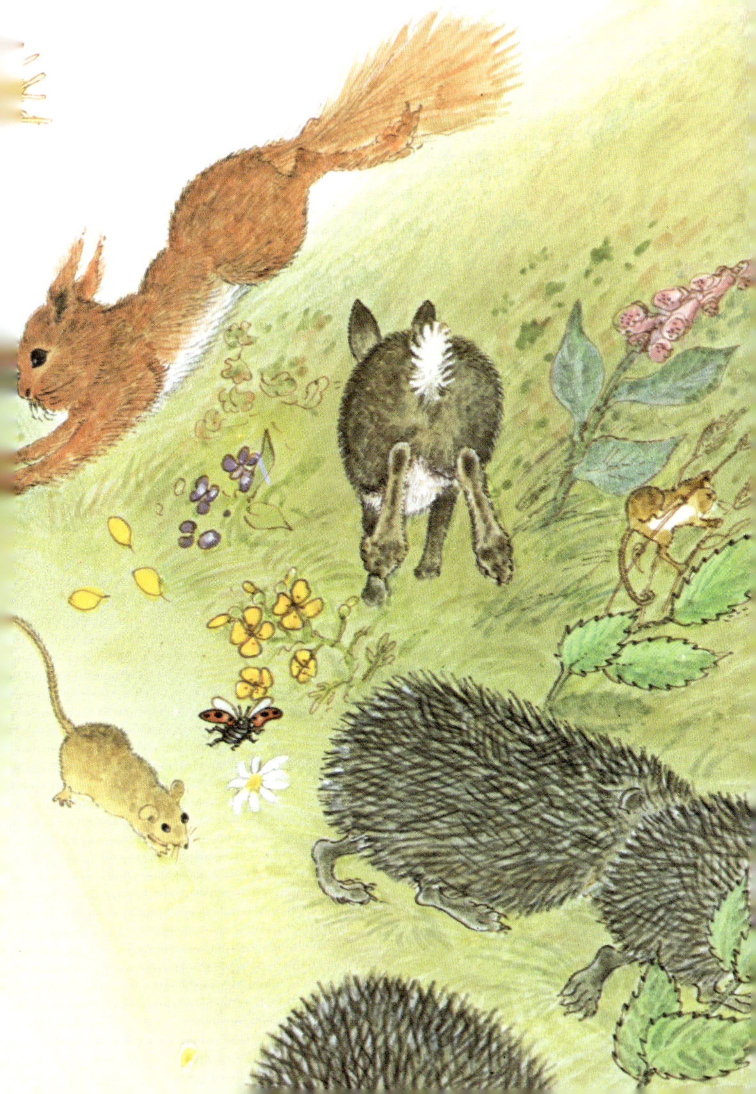

They held their breath
and closed their eyes.

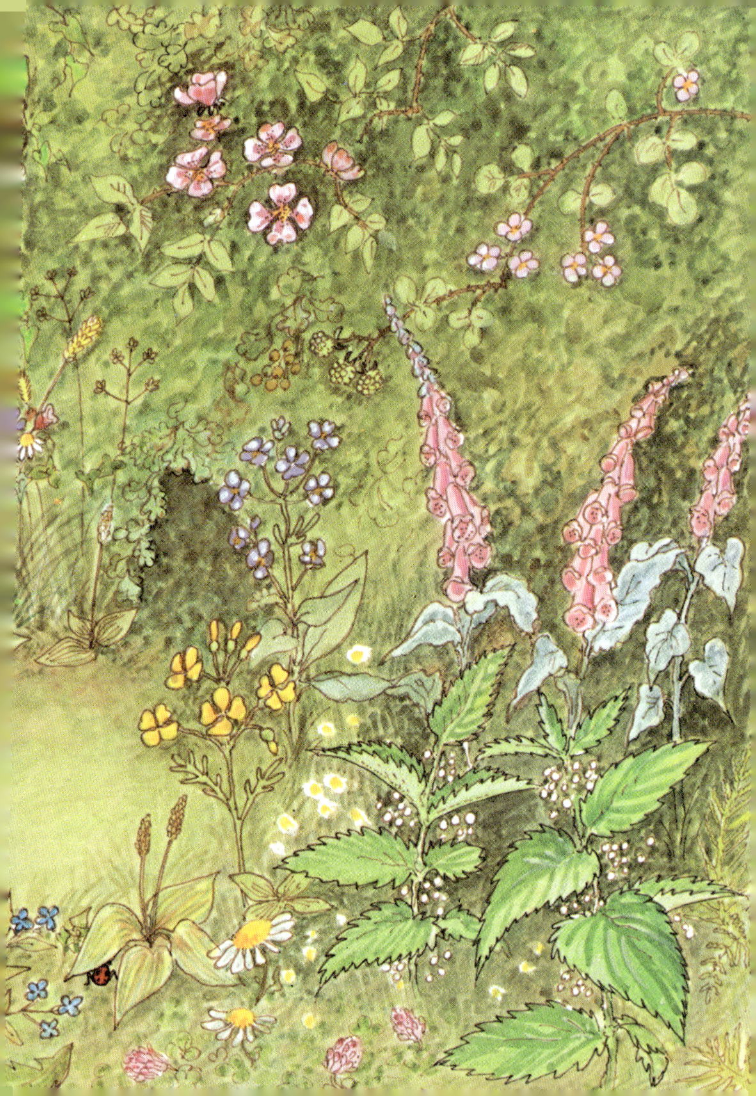

Clomp!
Down came one very large,
very muddy gumboot.

Stomp!
Down came another very large,
very muddy gumboot.

Clomp, stomp! Clomp, stomp!
Clomp, clump.
The footsteps faded away.
Everyone opened their eyes.
They hardly dared to look.
"Oh no," squeaked the hedgehogs,
"The stage is squashed to bits."

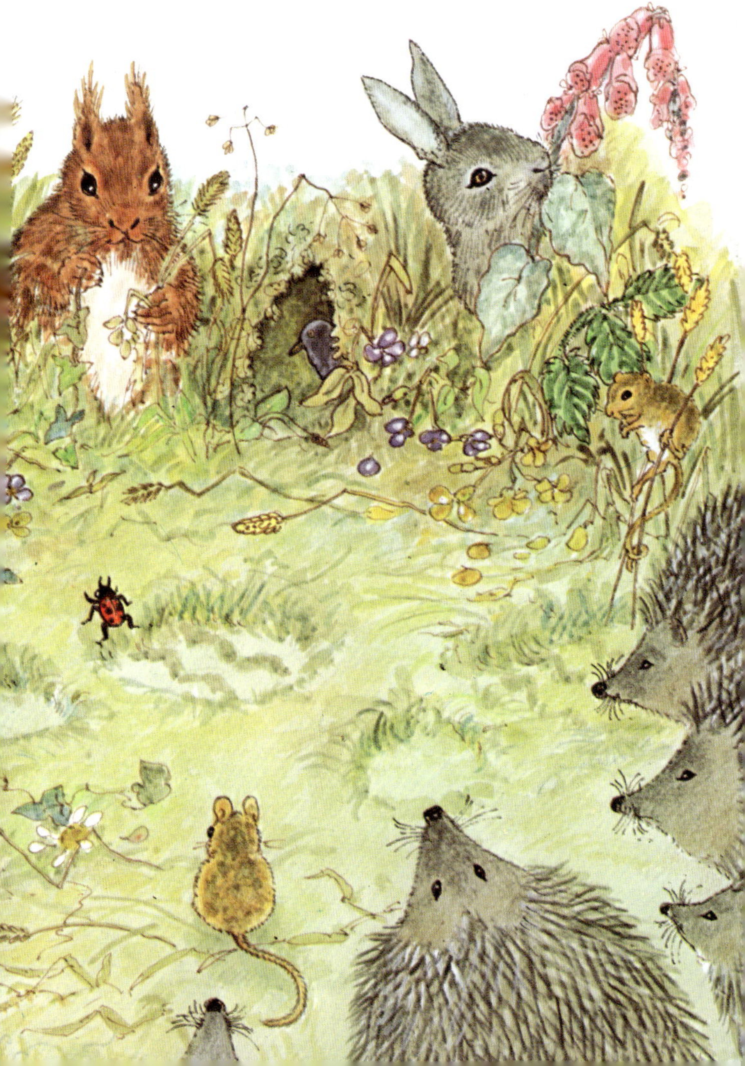

"But our feast is all right," twittered the birds.
"Hooray!" cheered everybody.
"Time to eat."

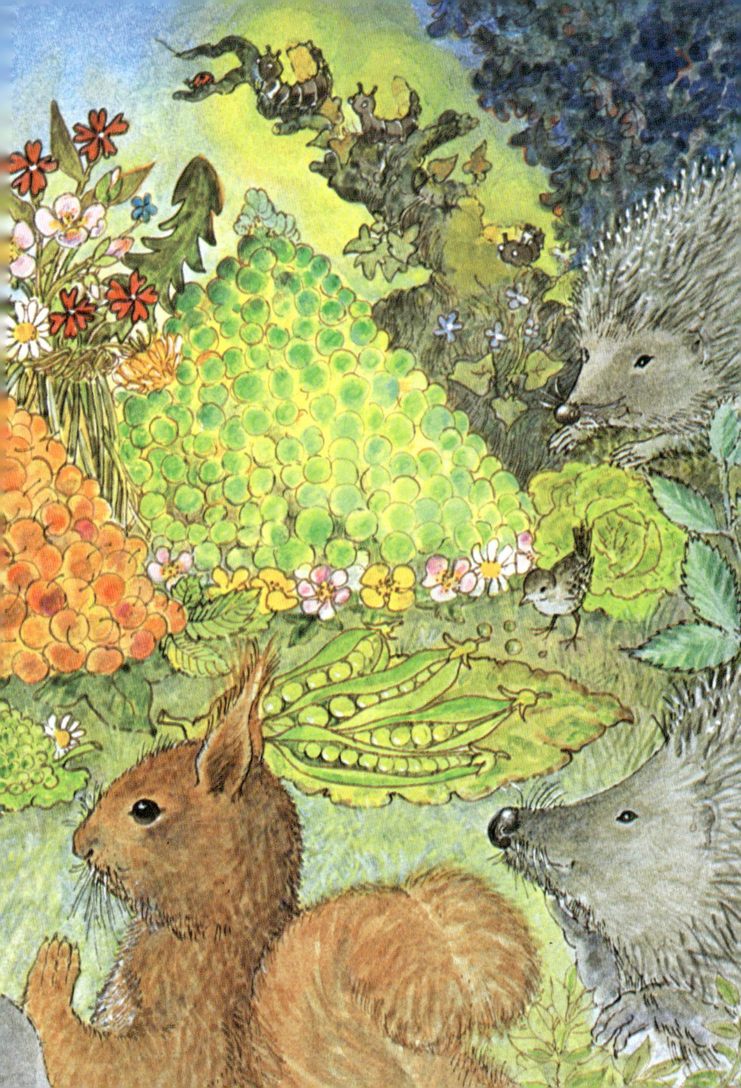

By the gleam of the glow-worms everyone feasted . . .

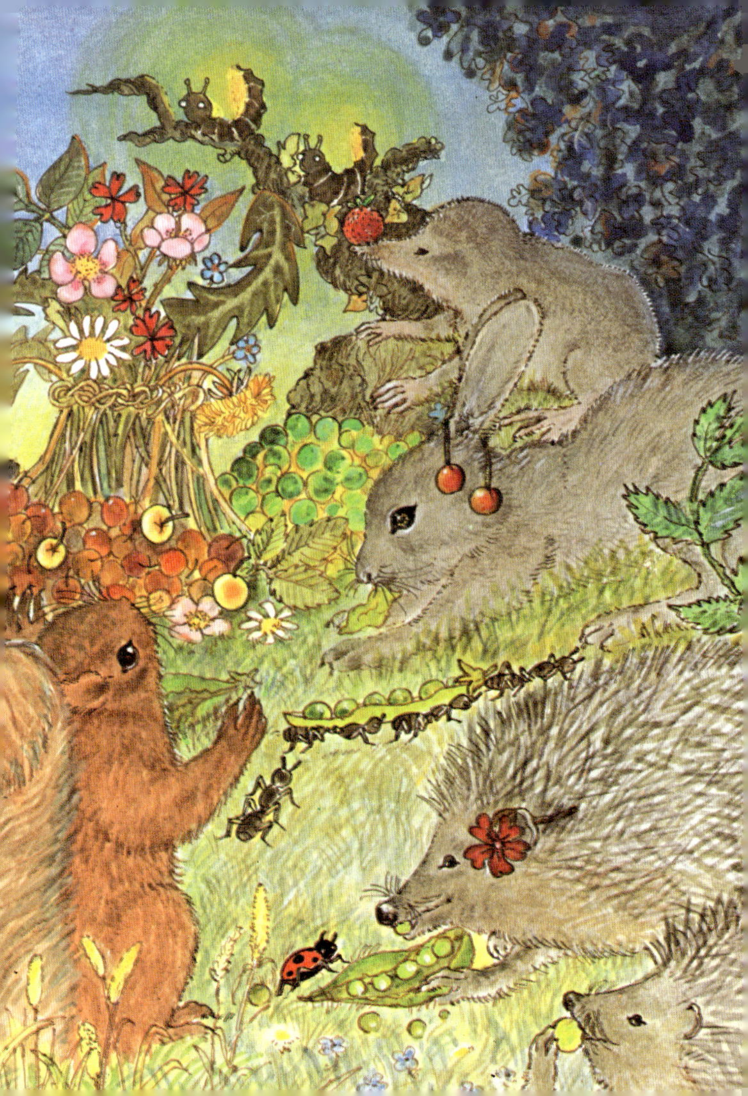

until they could eat no more.

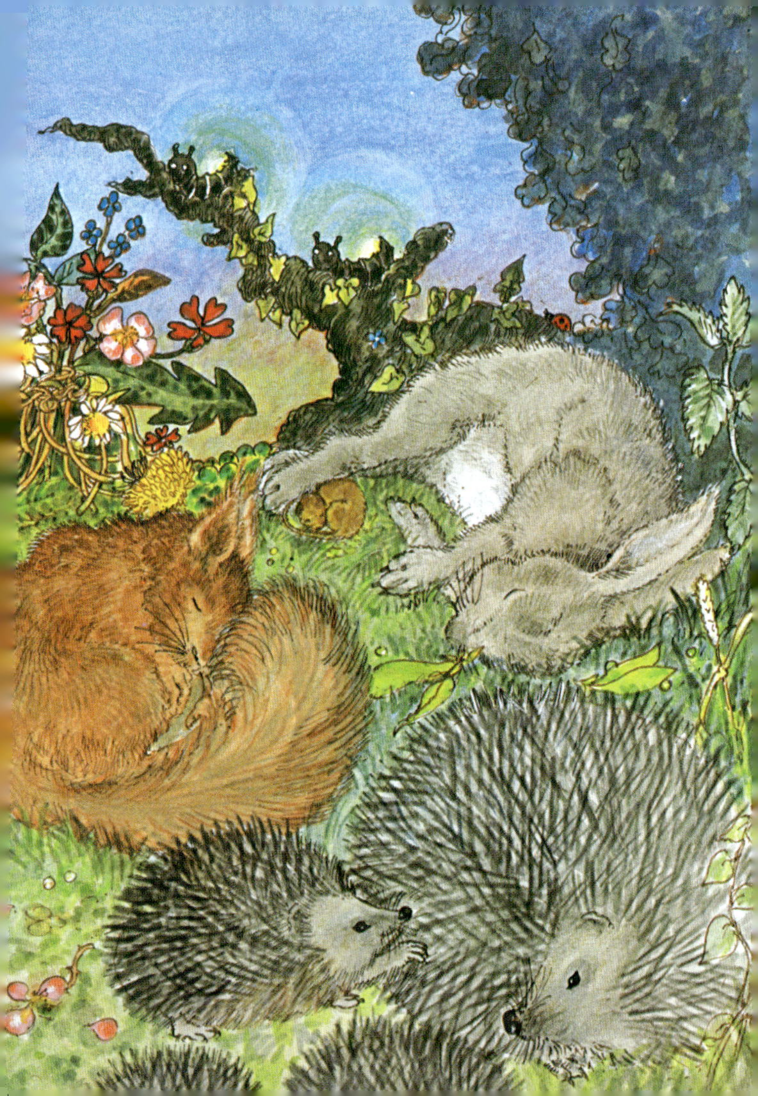

And the hedgehogs had their turn after all!

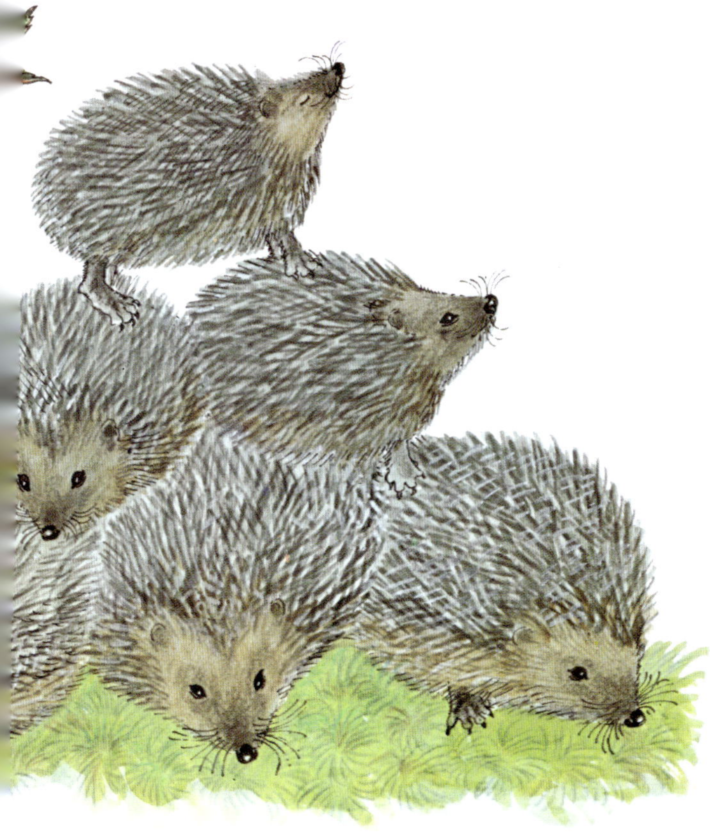

MY NATURE LIBRARY

First Edition Copyright © 1982
The Reader's Digest Association
Limited, Berkeley Square House,
Berkeley Square, London W1X 6AB
Reprinted 1992

All rights reserved

® READER'S DIGEST, THE DIGEST and
the Pegasus logo are registered trademarks of
The Reader's Digest Association, Inc.
of Pleasantville, New York, U.S.A.

Phototypeset by Tradespools Limited
Frome, Somerset
Printed in Hong Kong
40.133.5

A bird story

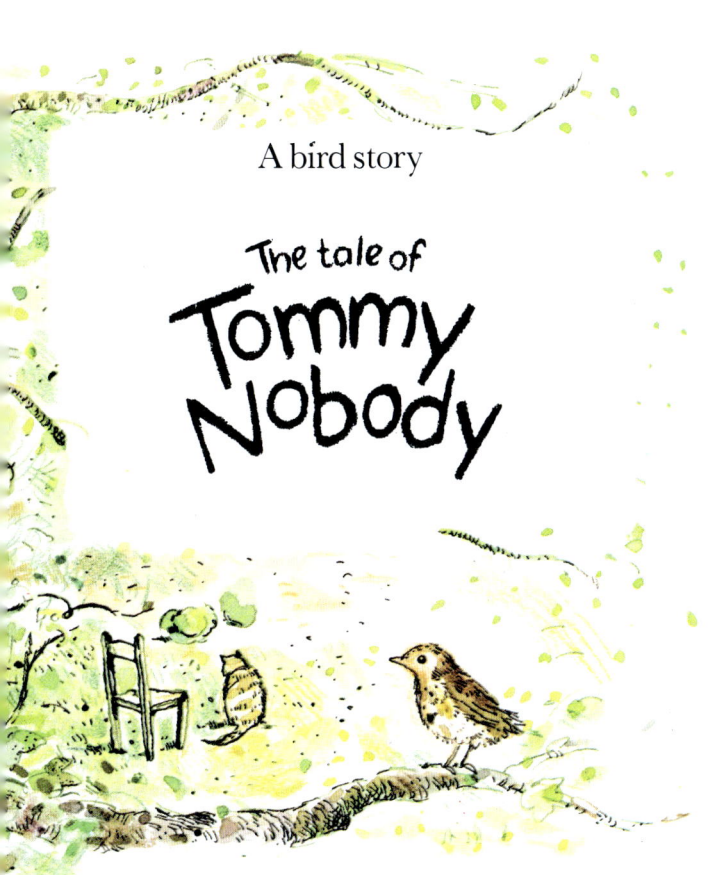

# The tale of Tommy Nobody

Written by Ruth Thomson
Illustrated by Charlotte Voake

PUBLISHED BY THE READER'S DIGEST ASSOCIATION LIMITED

Sally was as busy as could be.
It was spring again –
time for her to build a nest.
She chose a quiet tree
at the bottom of the garden.

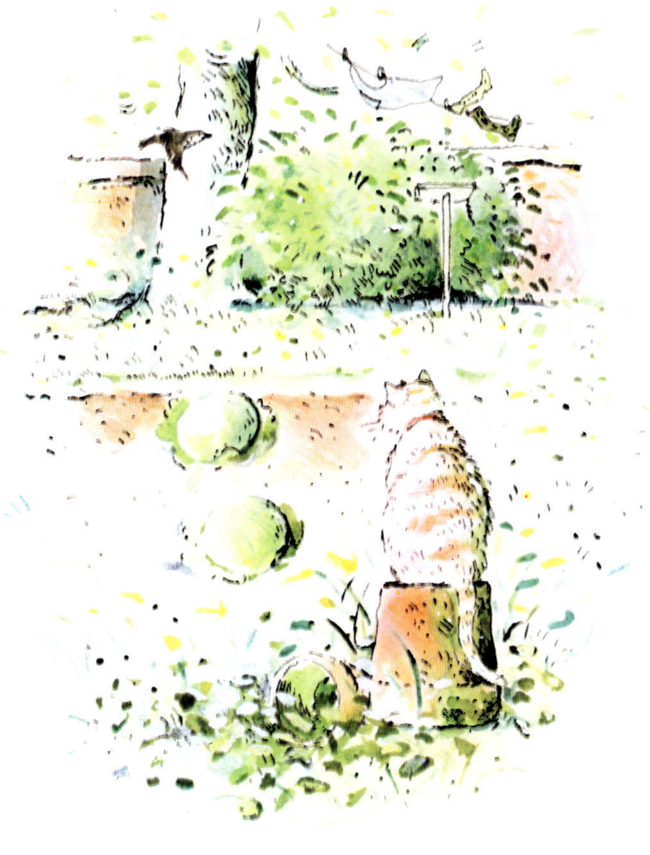

In and out she flew,
bringing all the grass and mud
she needed.

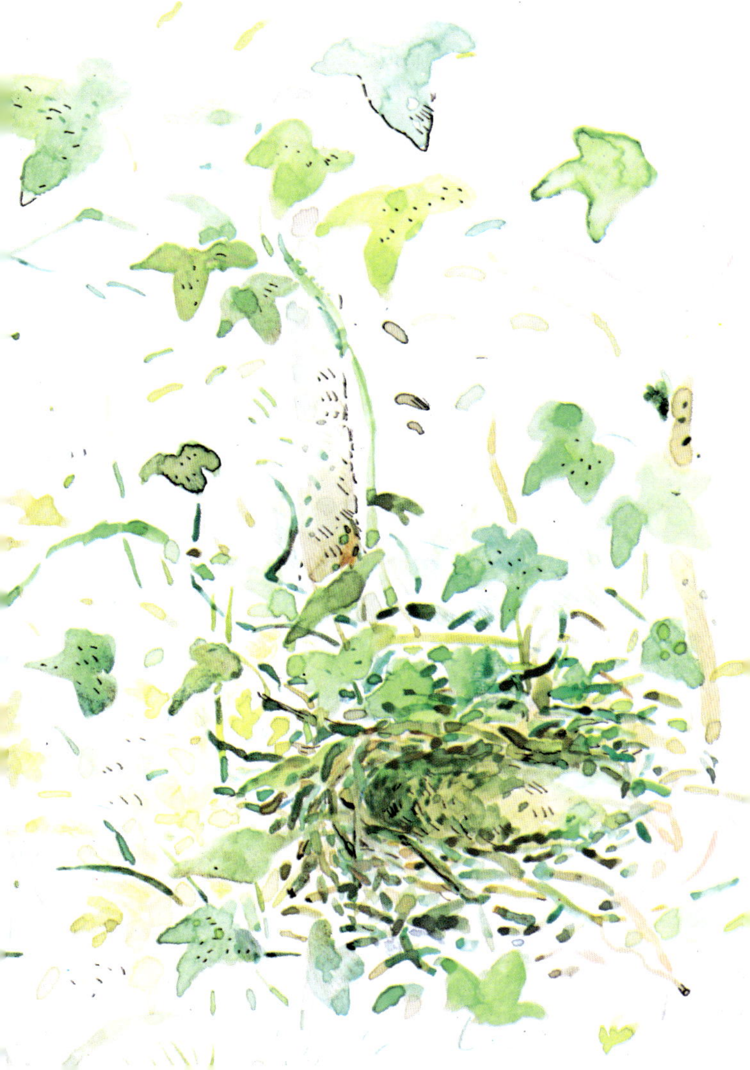

When the nest was quite ready,
Sally laid her eggs.
"One, two, three, four, five, six,"
she counted, "That's a fine number."

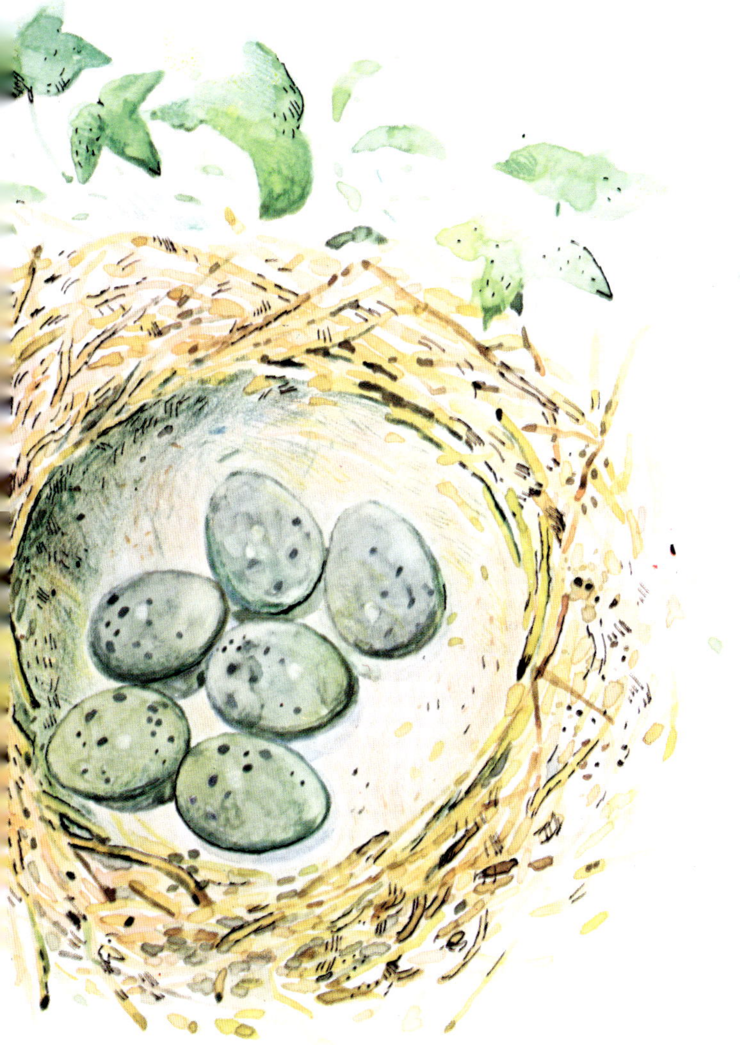

Proudly she sat on the nest,
keeping her eggs warm and safe.
Day after day she sat there
until the eggs were ready to hatch.

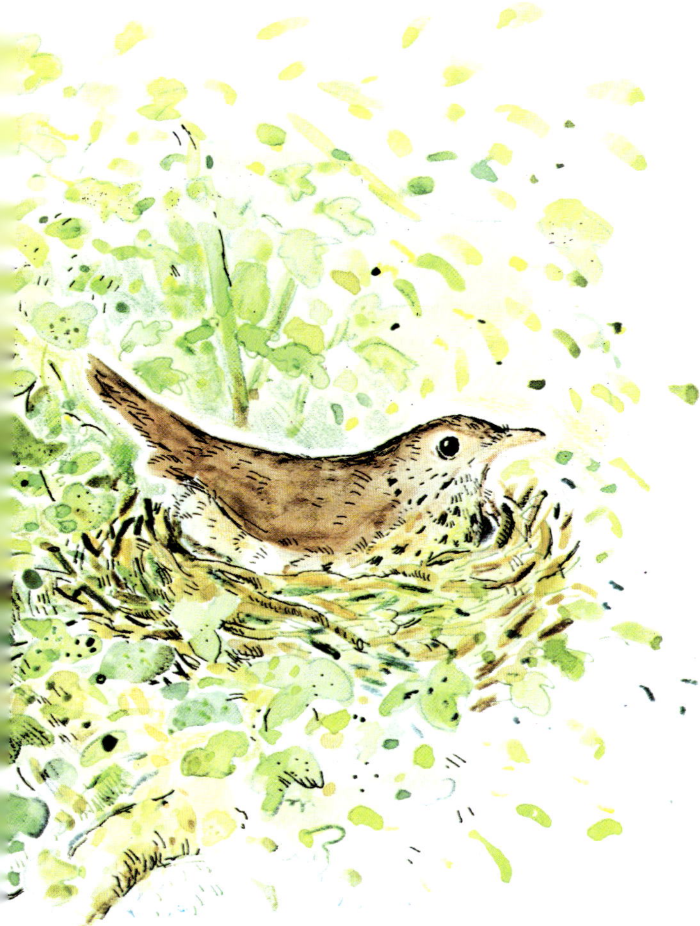

The tiny chicks opened their mouths and squawked for food.

"One, two, three, four, five, six,"
Sally counted with a sigh,
"That's a lot of mouths to feed."

Before long, the baby birds
were ready to learn to fly.
"One, two, three, four, five, six,"
counted Sally once more
as they sat on the edge
of the nest.
"Just checking."

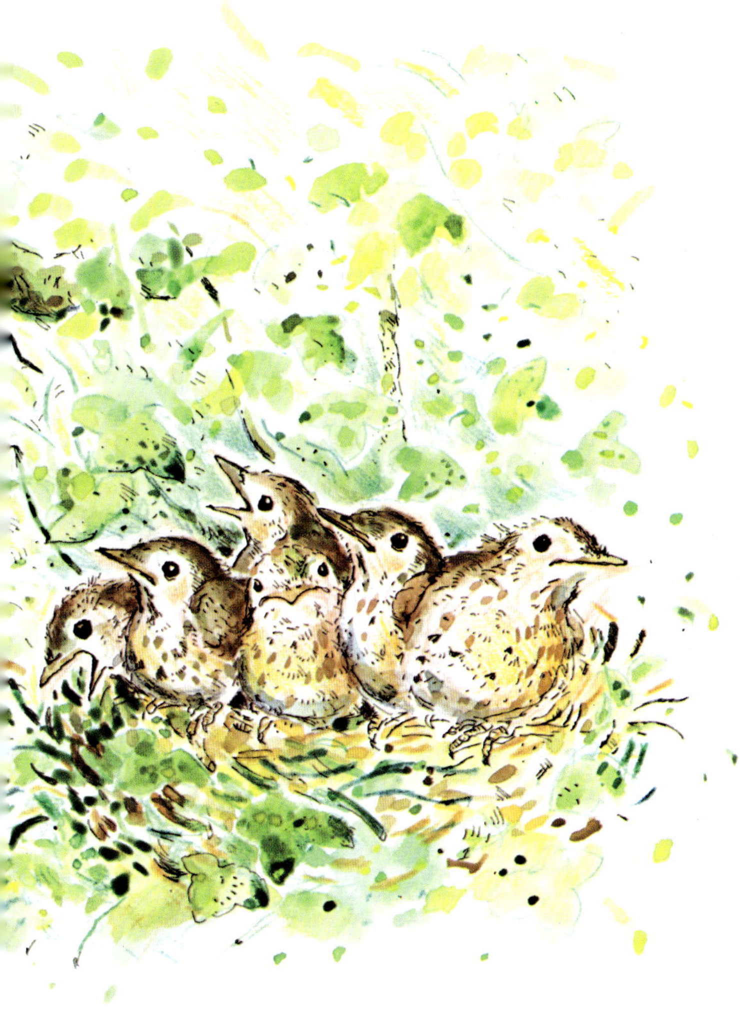

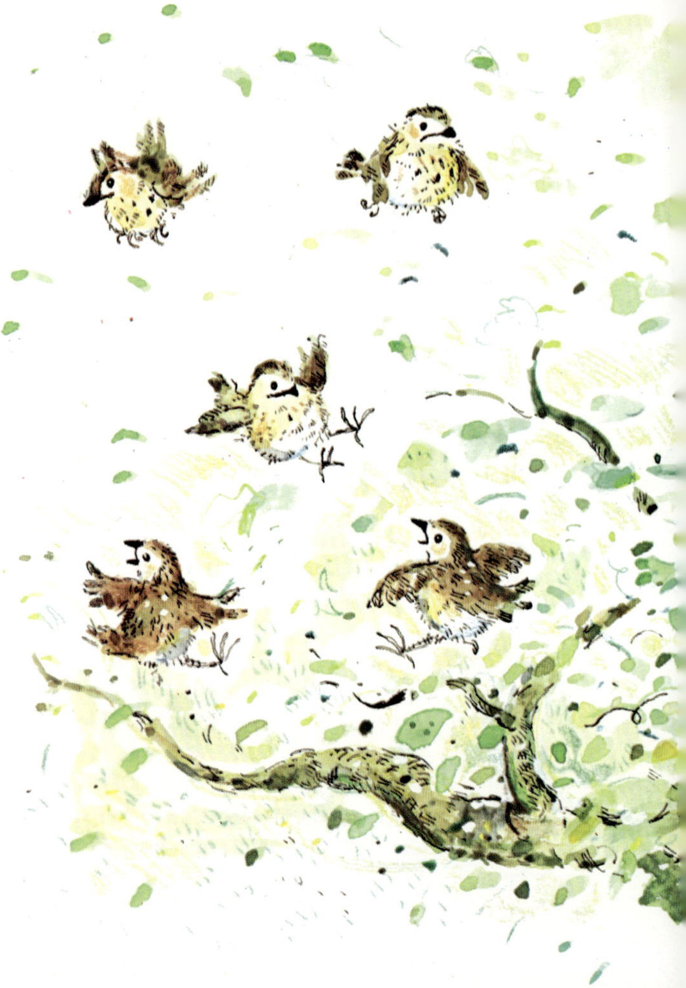

"Flap hard," called Sally
as they each took off in turn.
Tommy, the smallest, was the last
to go.

He could see that the other five
had landed safely
on a nearby branch.
They were watching him.

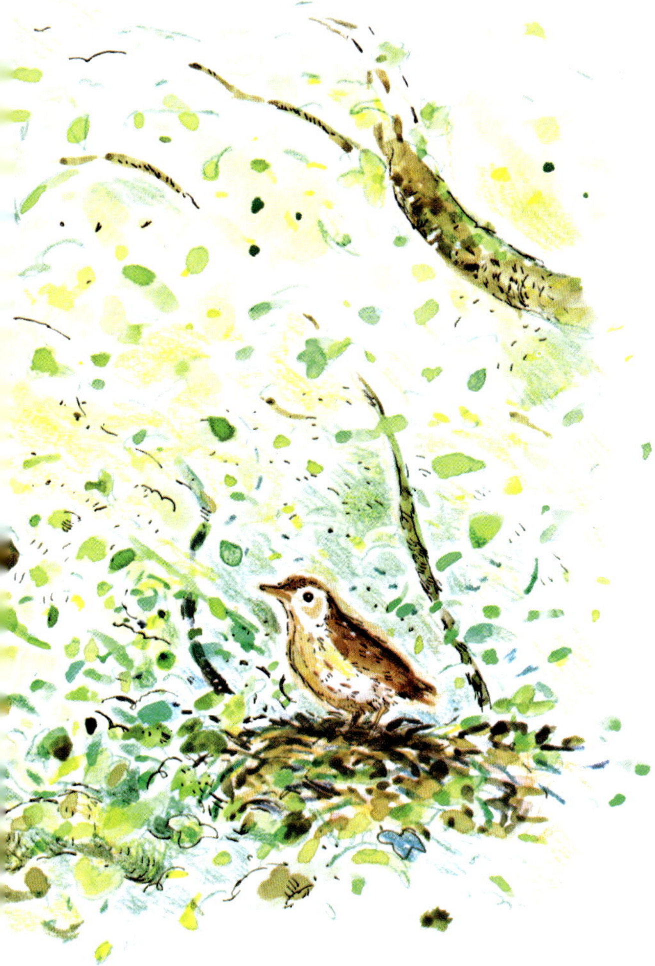

He flapped his wings wildly, but they didn't seem to work properly.
He could feel himself falling.

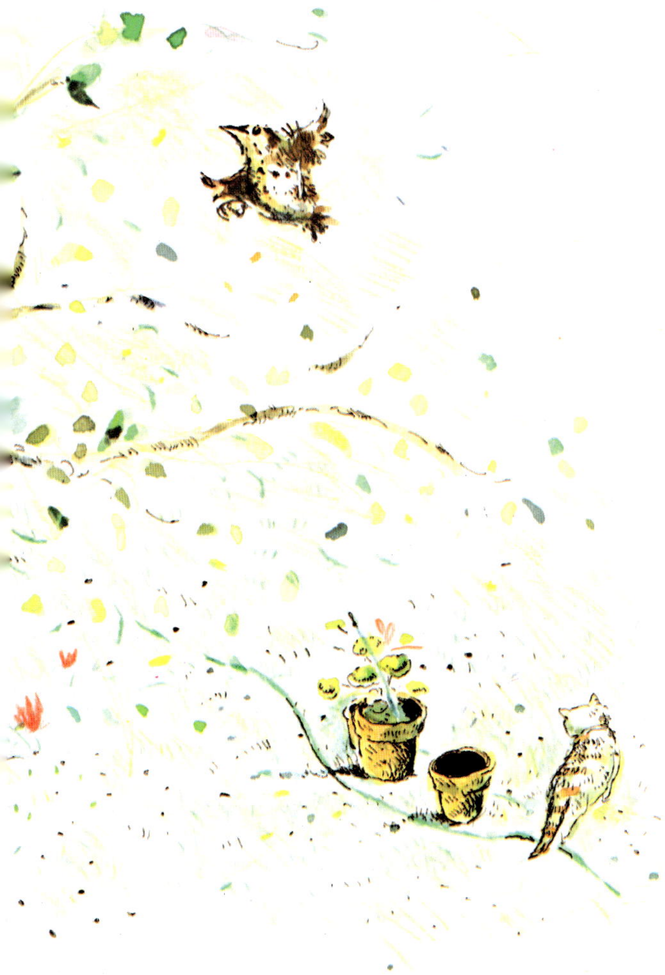

He flapped harder.
Out of the corner of his eye,
he could see below him
a very wide branch.
Lots of birds were sitting on it.

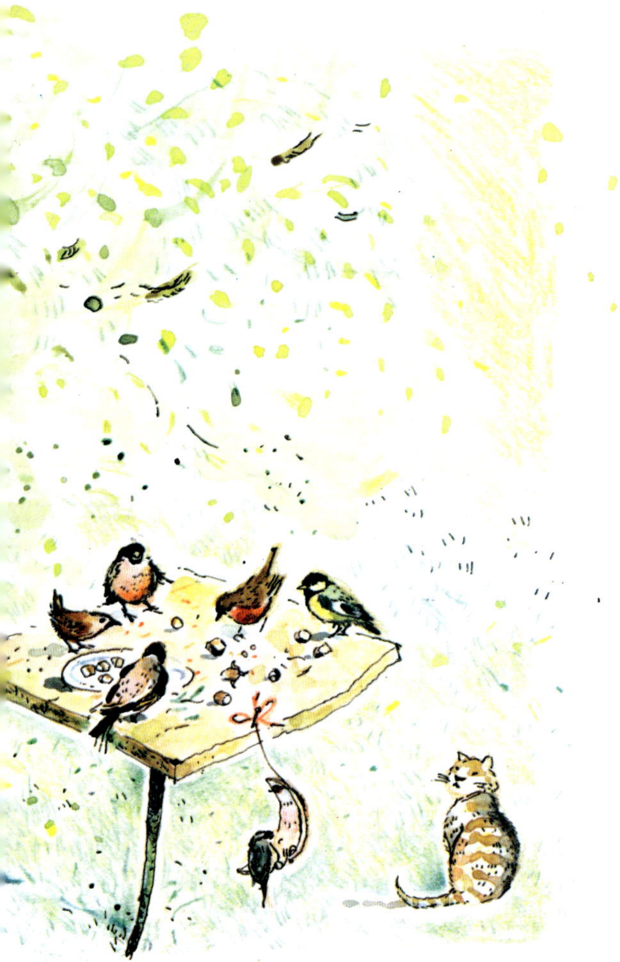

Splot!

Tommy landed with a crash
on a bird-table.
The birds all crowded round him.
"And what kind of bird are you,
may we ask?" they chorused.
"I really don't know,"
replied Tommy shyly.

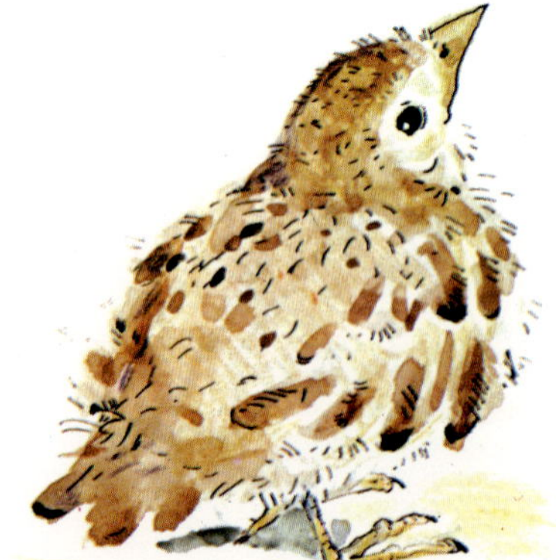

Bobby bullfinch bustled up.
"Everyone is somebody," he said.

"You'd better find out
what you are, or you won't know
what to do."
"I see," said Tommy meekly.

"Tic, tic," said Roger robin
beside him, proudly puffing out
his breast for Tommy to admire.
"Well, you can't be a robin,
for a start, because you don't have
a red breast like mine."

Tommy looked down at his own spotted chest and shook his head.

"Tit-tit-tit," called Jenny wren
bobbing busily behind Tommy.
"Can you cock your tail like this?"
Tommy tried, but he couldn't.
"Then you can't be a wren like me."

"Tee-tee-tee tisitisi," called
Billy bluetit from under the table.
"Can you do this?"

Tommy watched in amazement
as Billy hung upside-down
and pecked on a swinging coconut.
"I doubt it," said Tommy.
"Then you can't be a bluetit
like me."

"Tee-cher, tee-cher, move over,"
called George great tit,
pushing Tommy out of the way.
"I bet you can't do this,"
he said, and hammered at a nut
with his powerful bill.

"Indeed I can't," said Tommy after several tries.
"Then you can't be a great tit like me."

"Twitt-witt-witt," called Gerda goldfinch.
"Do you like thistles?"
Tommy took a mouthful of seeds, made a face and spat them out.

"I certainly do not," he said.
"Then you can't possibly be
a goldfinch like me.
Thistles are my favourite food."

Tommy wasn't like any of the birds
on the bird-table, so what was he?
He could see some other birds
on the ground.
"Perhaps I'm like one of those,"
he said to himself.

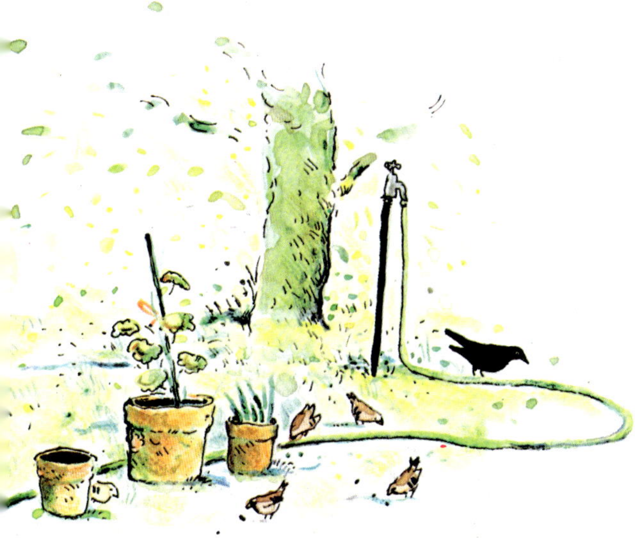

He took a deep breath,
leaped into the air
and flapped his wings.
Plop!
He landed fair and square in a puddle.

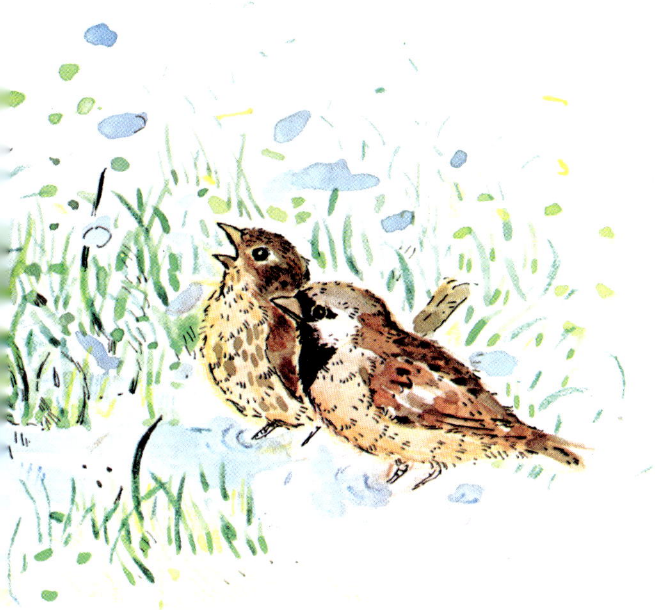

"Cheep, cheep," twittered
the sparrows, splashing
in another puddle nearby.
"Have you come for a bathe?"
they asked.
"Definitely not," said Tommy,
shaking himself dry.

"I came to see if I was a sparrow like you."
"You can't be a sparrow
if you don't like bathing.
We like bathing almost as much
as eating; and we eat anything!"

Tommy hopped over to a tree
where he could hear a loud noise.
"Can I help you?" called down
a spotted woodpecker.

"Do you think I might be a bird
like you?" Tommy asked.
"Only if you can do this,"
said the woodpecker, drumming
against the tree trunk.
Tommy tried, but just hurt his bill.
"Then you can't be a woodpecker
like me."

Tommy went to see Barney blackbird who was pulling up a worm.
He told Barney his story.

Barney looked him up and down. "Well," he said, "You do look a bit like me, but you're the wrong colour for a blackbird."

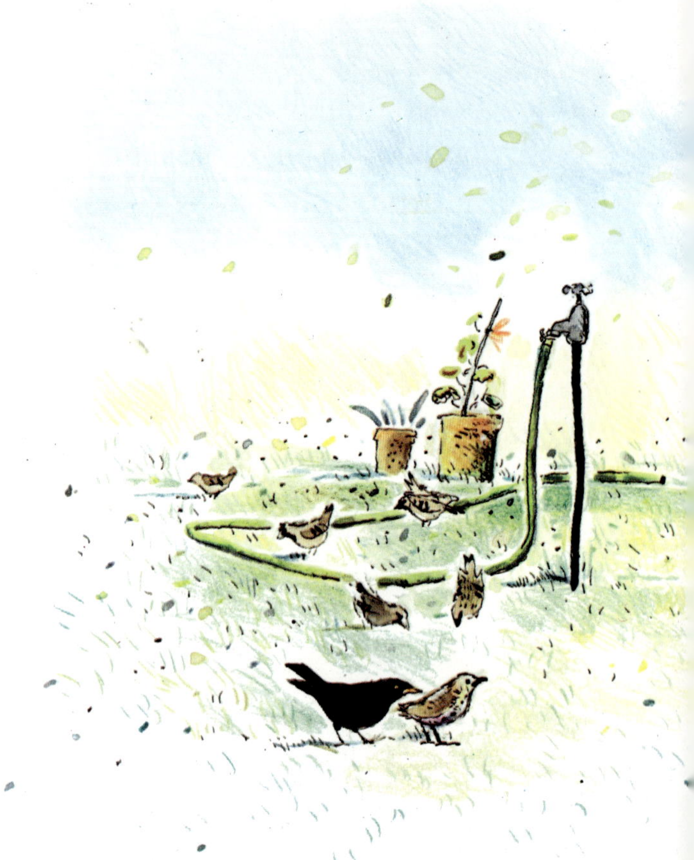

Just then, a small flock
of starlings landed on the lawn.

They started to eat the bread
that had been put out
for the other birds.

They squabbled and fought
so much, they scared away
all the other birds.
All except Tommy.

"Well," said a bossy starling
to Tommy, "What do you want?"
"I . . . I was wondering if I was
a starling like you."
"No chance," said the starling
very rudely.

"Just look at my shiny black feathers. You're all dull and drab. Besides, you can't copy the hoot of a tawny owl, now can you?" Tommy had nothing to say.

He ran across the lawn
away from the horrid starlings.
On the path at the end,

he came across a very busy bird.
It was banging a snail shell
on a stone.

"What are you doing?"
asked Tommy.
"Having breakfast,"
replied the bird.
"I wonder if you could help me,"
asked Tommy most politely.
"Am I the same sort of bird
as you?"

"There's only one way
to find out," said the bird.
"Can you sing?"

"I don't know," said Tommy,
"I've never tried."
The other bird began to sing –
long, high, rich notes.
Tommy opened his mouth and sang;
quietly at first,
then louder and louder.

He could sing!
"You're like me all right,"
said the other bird.
"I'm a songthrush and so are you."

"A songthrush!" exclaimed Tommy.
Forgetting all his fears,
he took off in excitement.
Higher and higher he flew,
right to the very top
of an apple tree.
There he sang his heart out,
glad to be Tommy Somebody at last.

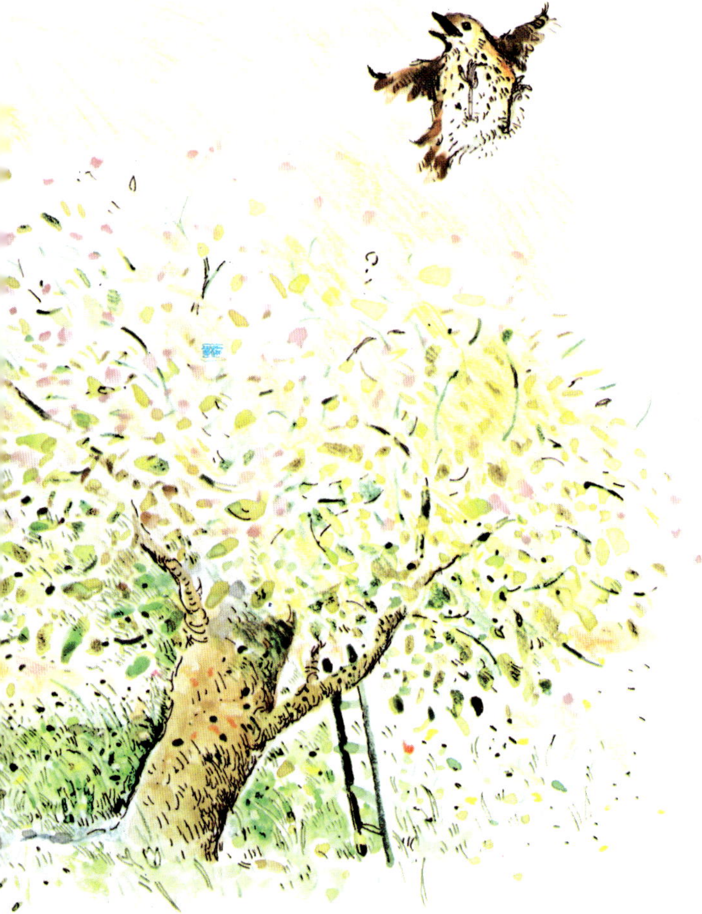

# MY NATURE LIBRARY

First Edition Copyright © 1982
The Reader's Digest Association
Limited, Berkeley Square House,
Berkeley Square, London W1X 6AB
Reprinted 1992

All rights reserved

® READER'S DIGEST, THE DIGEST and
the Pegasus logo are registered trademarks of
The Reader's Digest Association, Inc.
of Pleasantville, New York, U.S.A.

Phototypeset by Tradespools Limited
Frome, Somerset
Printed in Hong Kong
40.133.5

Nature rhymes and verses

# worms wiggle, bugs jiggle

Edited by Ruth Thomson
Illustrated by Iris Schweitzer

PUBLISHED BY THE READER'S DIGEST ASSOCIATION LIMITED

JUMP OR JIGGLE

Frogs jump
Caterpillars hump

Worms wiggle
Bugs jiggle

Rabbits lop
Horses clop

Snakes slide
Sea-gulls glide

Mice creep
Deer leap

Puppies bounce
Kittens pounce

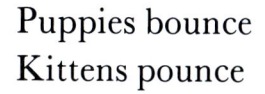

Lions stalk —
But —
I *walk*!

EVELYN BEYER

### THE PUSSY-WILLOW

The pussy-willow's bloom is soft,
Soft as my pussy's paws,
And pussy-willows do not scratch,
They have not any claws.

We gather branches in the spring,
And see the shining gold
Of little paws along the stem –
So furry-like to hold!

ALICIA ARMER

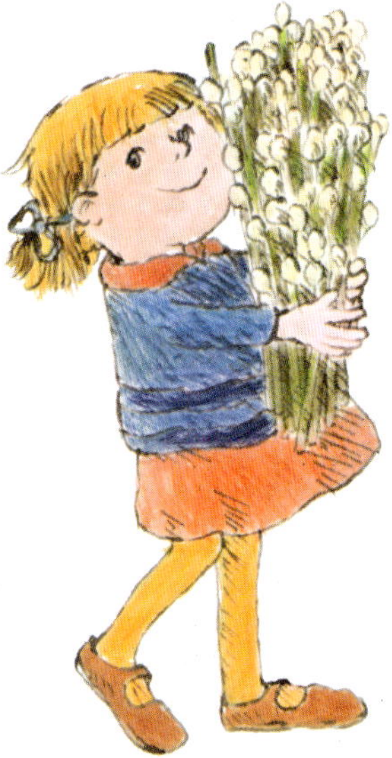

## MY GARDEN

Rabbits and moles
Always makes holes.

It's a rabbit habit.

But the moles should be told
That my lawn is all-holed.

BARBARA IRESON

## MOLES

Don't you feel sorry
for grubby old moles,
always in tunnels,
always in holes,
never out watching
the sun climb high
or the grass bend low
or the wind race by
or stars make twinkles
all over the sky?

AILEEN FISHER

## A WISE OLD OWL

A wise old owl sat in an oak,
The more he heard the less he spoke;
The less he spoke the more he heard,
Why aren't we all like that wise
   old bird?

TRADITIONAL

## THE CUCKOO

Seldom seen yet often heard
The cuckoo is an idle bird.
It lays its egg in another's nest,
The foster parents do the rest.

LESLEY CHURCHMAN

## BUZZY OLD BEES

There wouldn't be apples
on apple trees,
or daisies or clover
or such as these,
if it weren't for fuzzy old
buzzy old bees,
dusting pollen
from off their knees
on apple blossoms,
on apple trees,
and clover and daisies
and such as these.

**AILEEN FISHER**

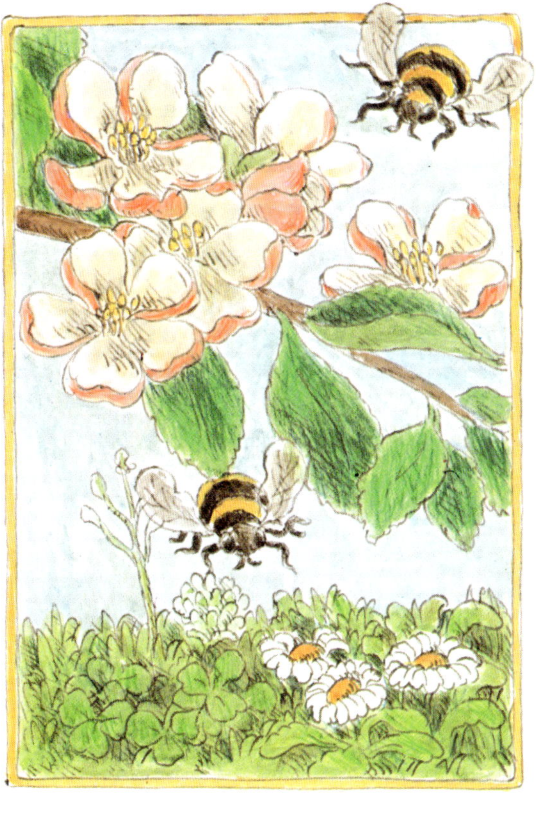

# THE CITY MOUSE AND THE GARDEN MOUSE

The city mouse lives in a house;
The garden mouse lives in a bower,
He's friendly with the frogs and
 toads,
He sees the pretty plants in
 flower.

The city mouse eats bread and cheese;
The garden mouse eats what he can;
We will not grudge him seeds and
   stalks,
Poor little, timid furry man.

CHRISTINA ROSSETTI

**THE TADPOLE**

Underneath the water-weeds
Small and black, I wriggle,
And life is most surprising!
Wiggle! waggle! wiggle!
There's every now and then a most
Exciting change in me,

I wonder, wiggle! waggle!
What I *shall* turn out to be!

E. E. GOULD

## CONKERS

When chestnuts are hanging
Above the school yard,
They are little green sea-mines,
Spiky and hard.

But when they fall bursting
And all the boys race,
Each shines like a jewel
In a satin case.

CLIVE SANSOM

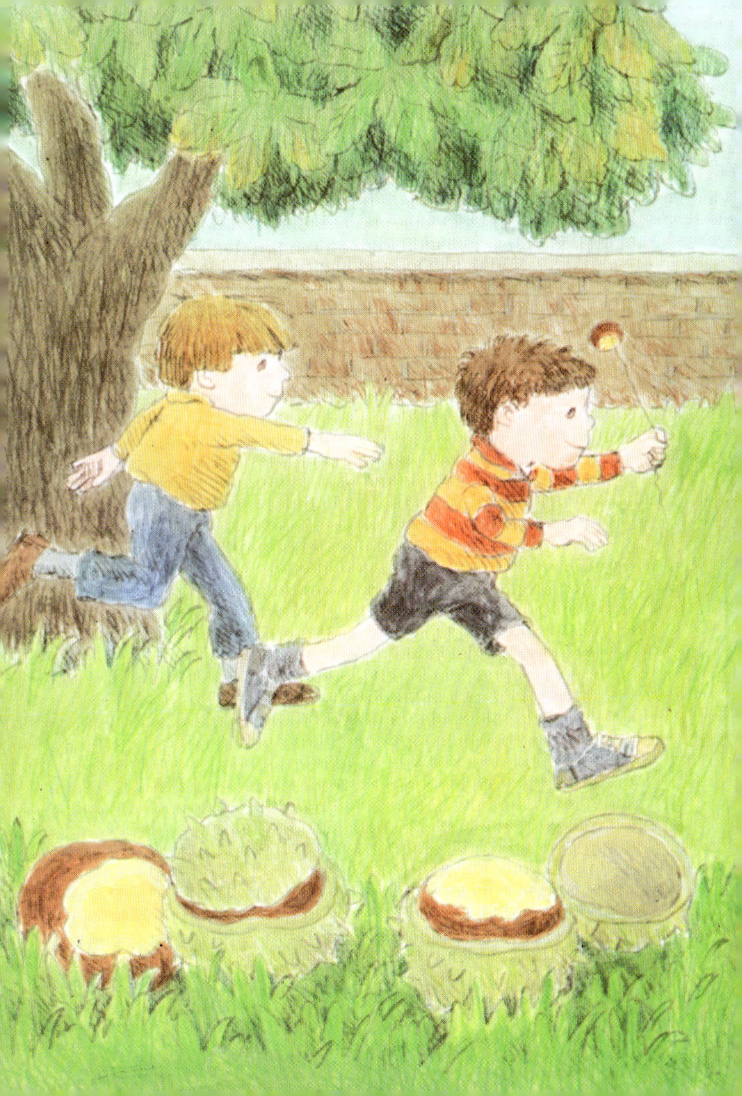

## TOM-TIT

I know a Tom-tit,
Swinging on a coconut,
Swinging on a coconut,
   that swings upon a tree.
Eating of his breakfast,
Pecking at a coconut,
Upside-down or anyhow,
   and busy as a bee.

He's blue and yellow,
Like a little harlequin,
Spick and span, a tit-mouse
   most elegant to see;
Outside the window,
Swinging on a sycamore,
Busy with his coconut,
   he don't mind me.

JOHN DRINKWATER

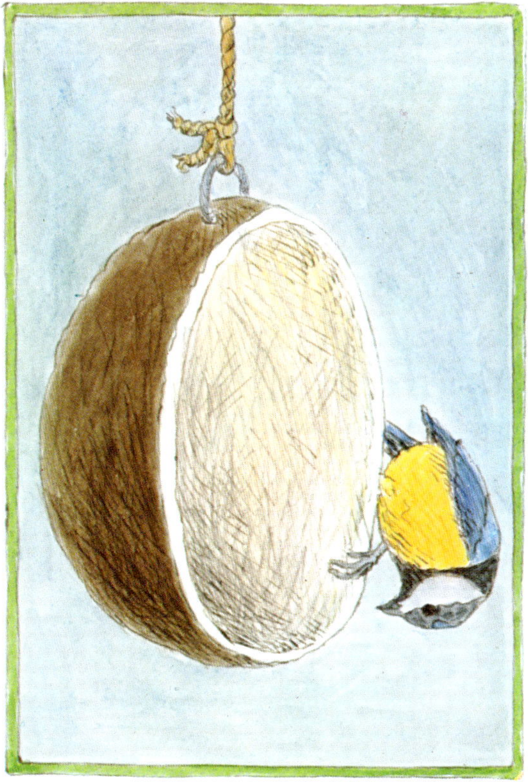

**BUTTERFLIES**

Dancing, fluttering
Carelessly by
Under the gleaming
Summer sky,
They haunt the grasses,
Light as air,
Rising here
And dipping there.

Meadow Brown,
Red Admiral,
Peacock and
Bright Tortoiseshell –
All so splendid
As they dance by
Under the sunlit
Summer sky!

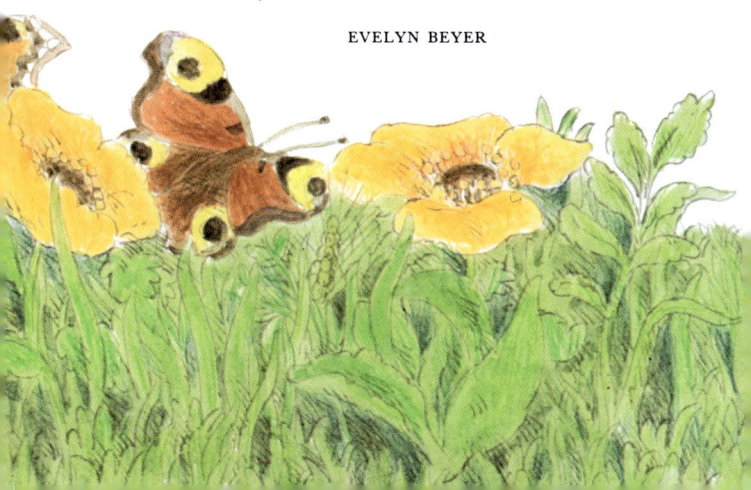

EVELYN BEYER

**THE DANDELION PUFF**

The dandelion puff
Is a very queer clock,
It doesn't say tick,
And it doesn't say tock,
It hasn't a cuckoo,
It hasn't a chime,
And I really don't think
It can tell me the time!

MARY K. ROBINSON

## DAISIES

Where innocent bright-eyed
daisies are,
With blades of grass between,
Each daisy stands up like a star
Out of a sky of green.

CHRISTINA ROSSETTI

**POOR ROBIN**

The North wind doth blow,
And we shall have snow,
And what will poor robin do then,
   poor thing?
He'll sit in a barn,
To keep himself warm,
And hide his head under his wing,
   poor thing.

ANON

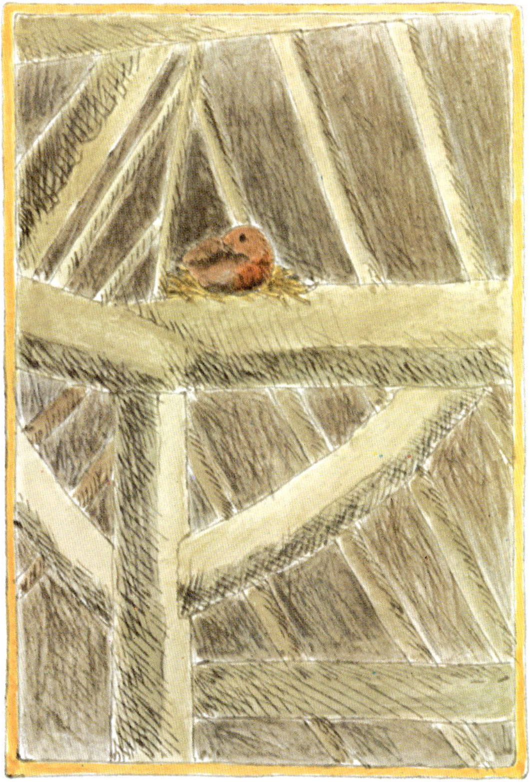

### SLUGS

Slugs, slugs
Crawl through grass,
Watching all the beetles
As they scurry past.

Slugs, slugs
Crawl so slow,
Leaving tracks of silver
Wherever they go.

Slugs, slugs
Crawl all along the wall,
Popping little horns out,
Make no sound at all.

JOHN KITCHING

## SNAIL

Snail upon the wall,
Have you got at all
Anything to tell
About your shell?

Only this, my child –
When the wind is wild,
Or when the sun is hot,
It's all I've got.

JOHN DRINKWATER

## THE HEDGEHOG

The hedgehog is a little beast
Who likes a quiet wood,
Where he can feed his family
On proper hedgehog food.

He has a funny little snout
That's rather like a pig's,
With which he smells, like us,
  of course,
But also runts and digs.

He wears the queerest prickle coat,
Instead of hair or fur,
And only has to curl himself
To bristle like a burr.

He does not need to battle with
Or run away from foes,
His coat does all the work for him,
It pricks them on the nose.

EDITH KING

## INCEY WINCEY SPIDER

Incey Wincey Spider
Climbing up the spout;
Down came the rain
And washed the spider out:
Out came the sunshine
And dried up all the rain;
Incey Wincey Spider
Climbing up again.

TRADITIONAL

### DADDY LONGLEGS

Don't you think a daddy longlegs
has a lot of fun
using all those stilts to walk
and all those stilts to run?

AILEEN FISHER

## DUCKS' DITTY

All along the backwater,
Through the rushes tall,
Ducks are a-dabbling,
Up tails all!

Ducks' tails, drakes' tails,
Yellow feet a-quiver,
Yellow bills all out of sight
Busy in the river!

KENNETH GRAHAME

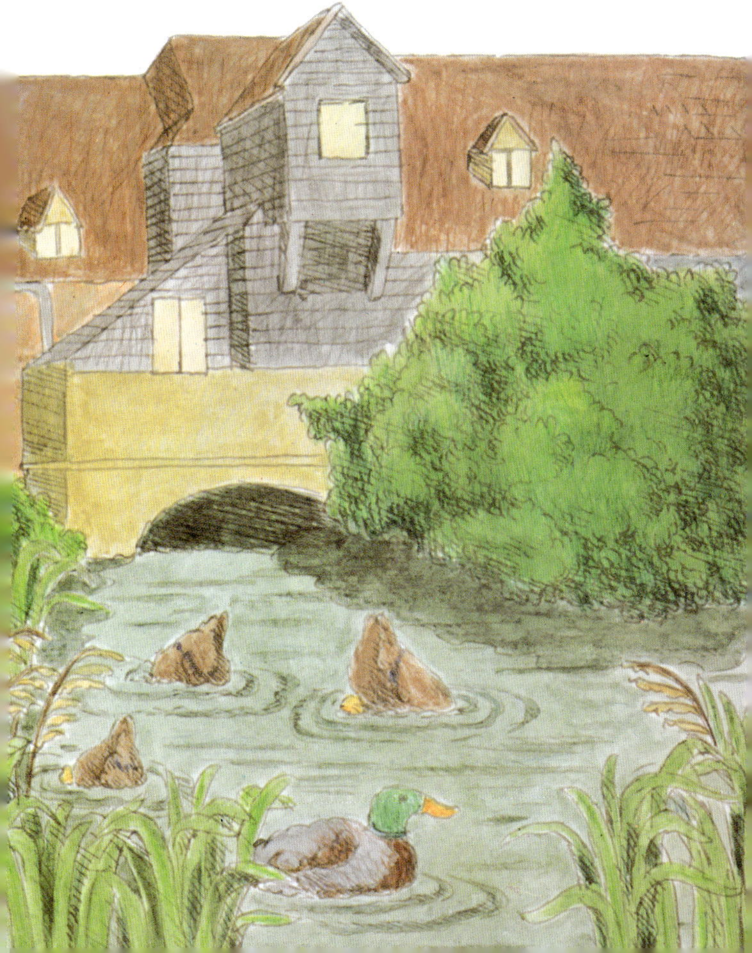

## GOLDEN GLORIES

The buttercup is like a golden cup,
The marigold is like a golden frill,
The daisy with a golden eye looks up,
And golden spreads the flag beside the rill,
And gay and golden nods the daffodil;
The gorsy common swells a golden sea,
The cowslip hangs a head of golden tips,
And golden drips the honey which the bee
Sucks from sweet hearts of flowers and stores and sips.

CHRISTINA ROSSETTI

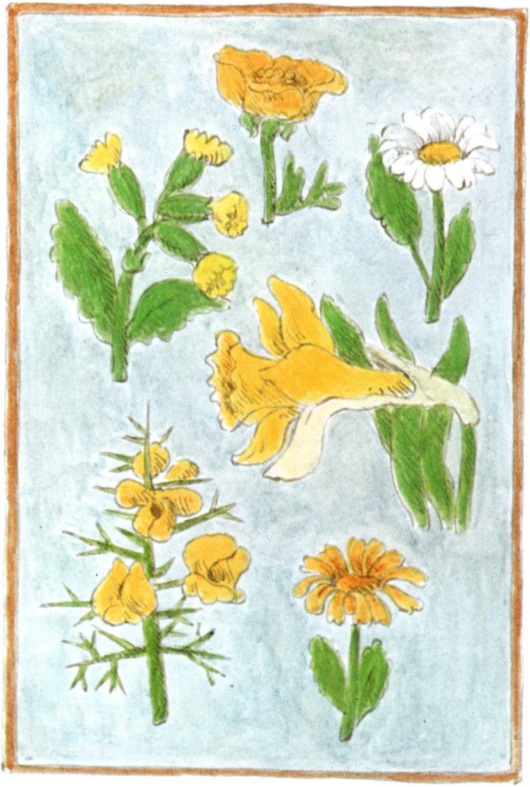

## A LITTLE BROWN RABBIT

A little brown rabbit popped out
  of the ground,
Wriggled his whiskers and looked
  around.
Another wee rabbit who lived
  in the grass
Popped his head out and watched
  him pass.
Then both the wee rabbits went
  hoppity, hop,

hoppity, hoppity, hoppity, hop,
Till they came to a wall and had
    to stop.
Then both the wee rabbits turned
    themselves round,
And scuttled off home to their holes
    in the ground.

TRADITIONAL

**LITTLE JENNY WREN**

As little Jenny Wren
Was sitting by the shed,
She waggled with her tail
And she nodded with her head.
She waggled with her tail
And she nodded with her head,
As little Jenny Wren
Was sitting by the shed.

TRADITIONAL

## BIRD BATH

There is a bird bath on our grass,
I wait to watch it as I pass,
And see the little sparrow things
Stand on the edge with flapping
   wings.
They give each eye a merry wink
And stoop to take a little drink,
And then, before I'm fairly gone,
They bath with all their clothing on!

FLORENCE HOATSON

ONLY MY OPINION

Is a caterpillar ticklish?
>   Well, it's always my belief
That he giggles, as he wiggles
>   Across a hairy leaf.

MONICA SHANNON

## THE MILLIPEDE

If millipedes wore shoes
Just think of all the fuss,
To do up all the laces
In time to catch the bus.

LESLEY CHURCHMAN

## TOADSTOOLS

It's not a bit windy,
It's not a bit wet,
The sky is as sunny
As summer, and yet
Little umbrellas are
Everywhere spread,
Pink ones, and brown ones,
And orange, and red.

I can't see the folks
Who are hidden below;
I've peeped and I've peeped
Round the edges, but no!
They hold their umbrellas
So tight and so close
That nothing shows under,
Not even a nose.

ELIZABETH FLEMING

### GREEN FROG

Bright-eyed, green frog,
Coloured like the grass;
Green, sheen-shining frog,
Leap when I pass.

Finish with your croaking,
Chunk-chunk, kerchunk!
Plunge into the water,
Plunk-plunk, kerplunk!

Swim below the water
To a sunken log;
Hide yourself, hide yourself,
Long-legged frog.

JAMES S. TIPPETT

## THE BROWN FROG

Today as I went out to play
I saw a brown frog in the way,
I know that frogs are smooth
   and green,
But this was brown – what could
   it mean?
I asked a lady in the road;
She said it was a spotted toad!

MARY K. ROBINSON

## WHISKY FRISKY

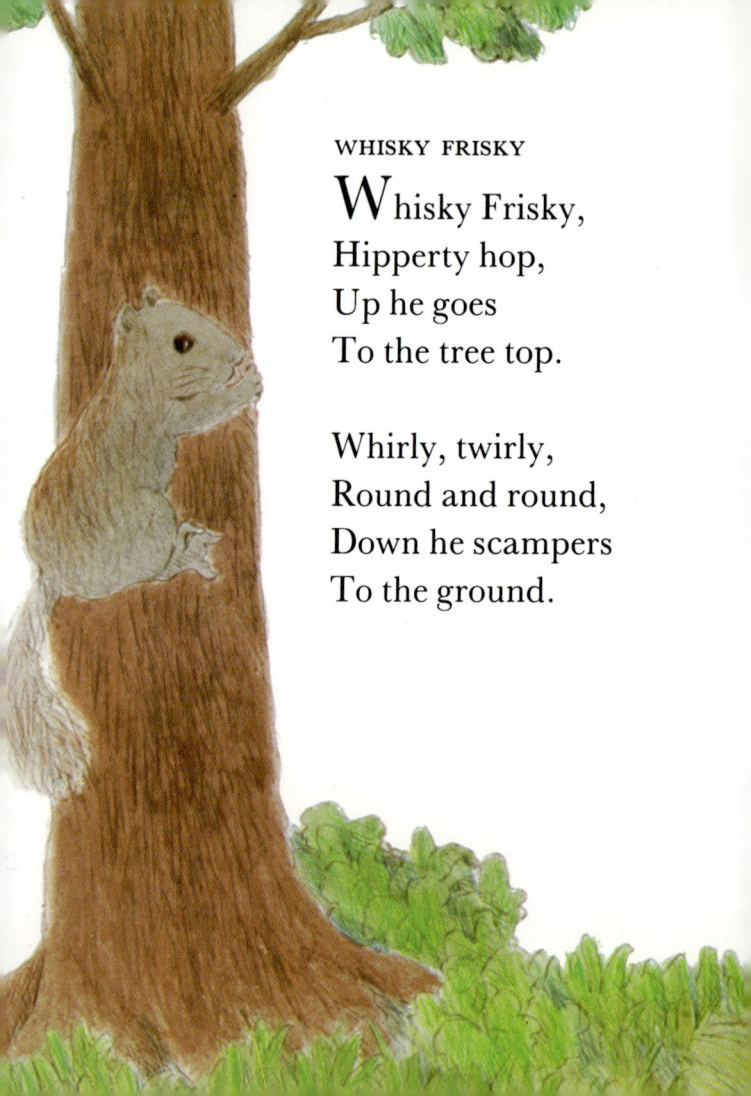

Whisky Frisky,
Hipperty hop,
Up he goes
To the tree top.

Whirly, twirly,
Round and round,
Down he scampers
To the ground.

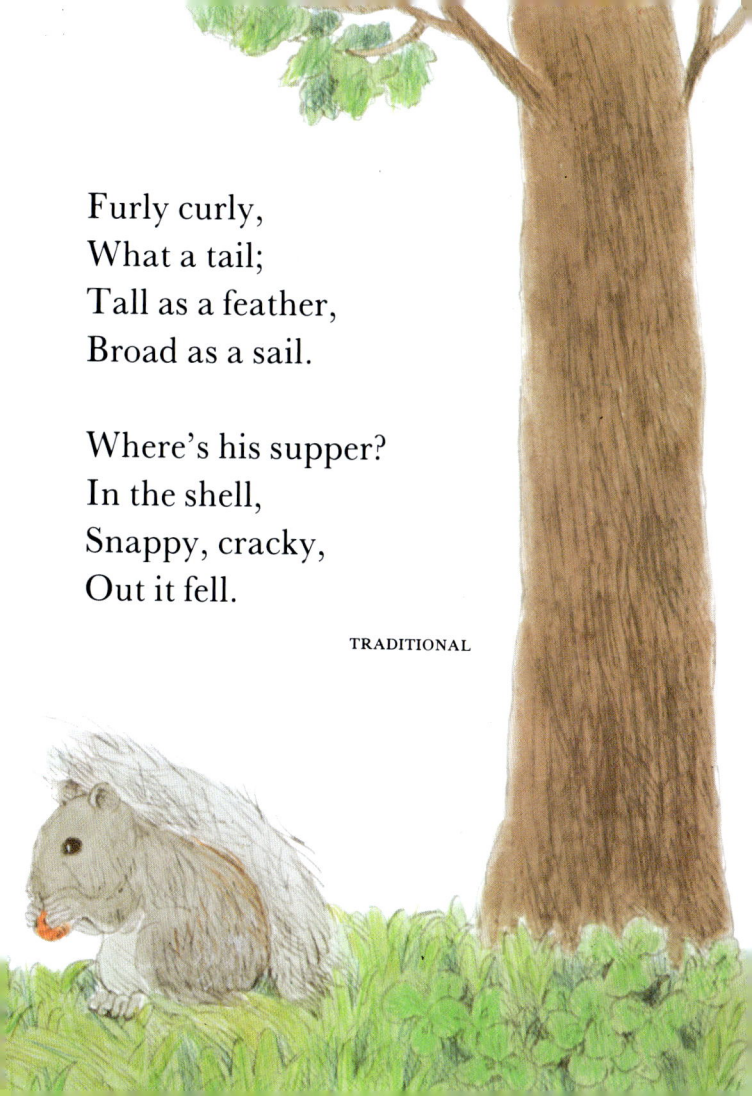

Furly curly,
What a tail;
Tall as a feather,
Broad as a sail.

Where's his supper?
In the shell,
Snappy, cracky,
Out it fell.

TRADITIONAL

## I HAD A LITTLE CHERRY STONE

I had a little cherry stone
And put it in the ground,
And when next year I went to look,
A tiny shoot I found.

The shoot grew upwards day by day,
And soon became a tree.
I picked the rosy cherries then,
And ate them for my tea.

BOYCE AND BARTLETT

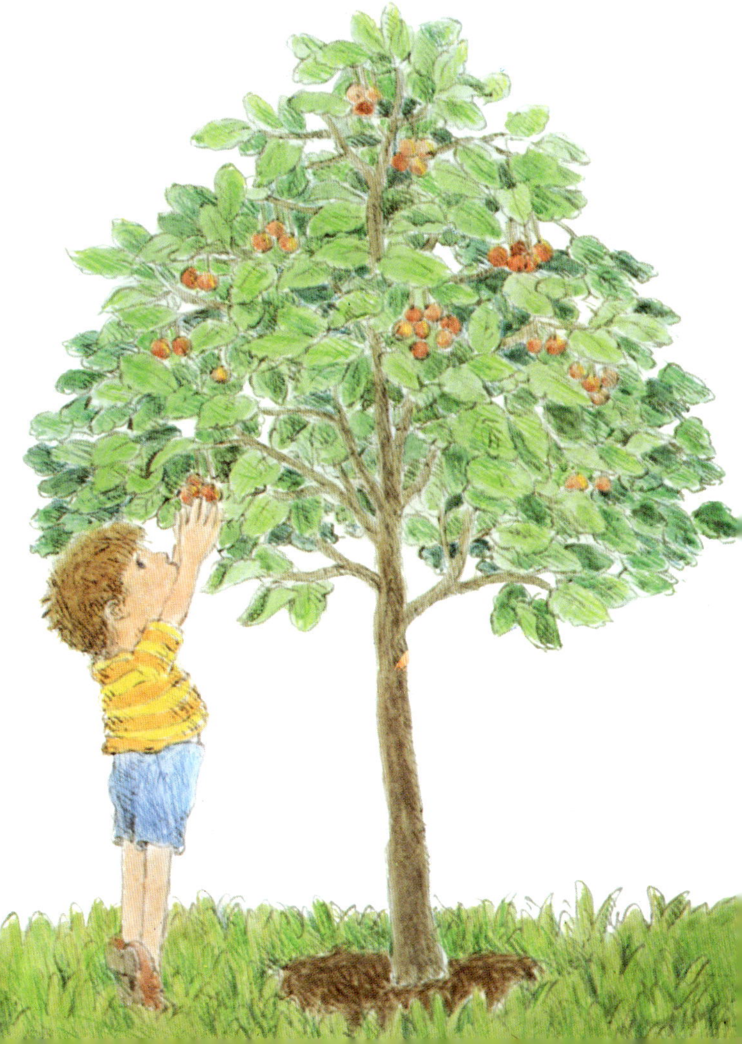

# GRASSHOPPER GREEN

Grasshopper Green is a comical chap;
He lives on the best of fare.
Bright little trousers, jacket and cap,
These are his summer wear.
Out in the meadow he loves to go,
Playing away in the sun;
It's hopperty, skipperty, high and low.
Summer's the time for fun!

TRADITIONAL

## THE CENTIPEDE

A centipede was happy quite,
Until a frog in fun
Said, 'Pray, which leg comes after which?'
This raised her mind to such a pitch,
She lay distracted in the ditch
Considering how to run.

TRADITIONAL

## UPSIDE DOWN

It's funny how beetles
and creatures like that
can walk upside down
as well as walk flat:

They crawl on a ceiling
and climb on a wall
without any practice
or trouble at all,

While I have been trying
for a year (maybe more)
and still I can't stand
with my head on the floor.

AILEEN FISHER

**EGGS ARE LAID BY TURKEYS**

Eggs are laid by turkeys
Eggs are laid by hens
Eggs are laid by robins
Eggs are laid by wrens

Eggs are laid by eagles
Eggs are laid by quail,
Pigeons, parrots, peregrines:
And that's how every bird begins.

MARY ANN HOBERMAN

## IN A WOOD

I like a wood. Wherever you go in it
There's always something you didn't know in it:

Roots and moss and gnarled bits of stick in it,
Shiny-backed beetles that hurry and kick in it;

Toadstools and fungus, grubs or a worm in it,
Odd little insects that scamper or squirm in it;

Dry leaves to shuffle in over your
shoes in it,
Wandering pathways to go where
you choose in it;

Always some nice sort of licheny
seat in it,
And mostly a nut or a berry to eat
in it;

An earthy and mossy and mildewy
smell in it –
Oh, hundreds more things than you
ever could tell in it!

JOYCE BRISLEY

### EXPLORERS

The furry moth explores the night,
The fish discover cities drowned,
And moles and worms and ants explore
The many cupboards underground.

The soaring lark explores the sky,
The gulls explore the stormy seas.
The busy squirrel rummages
Among the attics of the trees.

JAMES REEVES

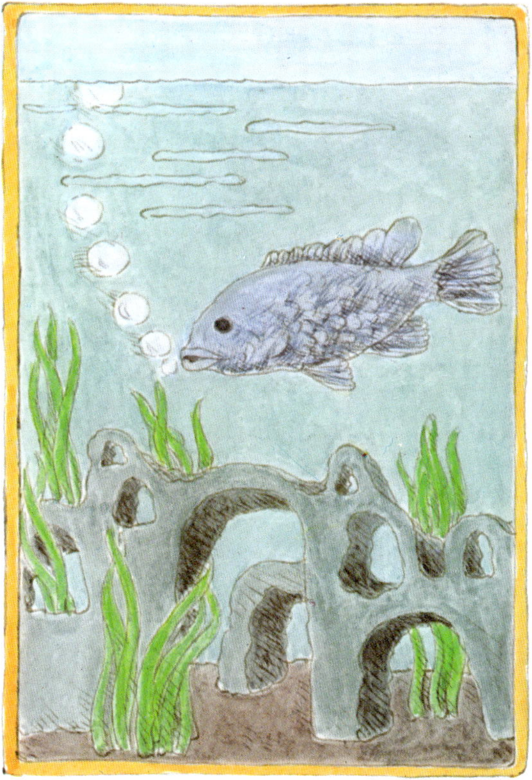

MY NATURE LIBRARY

First Edition Copyright © 1982
The Reader's Digest Association
Limited, Berkeley Square House,
Berkeley Square, London W1X 6AB
Reprinted 1992

All rights reserved

® READER'S DIGEST, THE DIGEST and
the Pegasus logo are registered trademarks of
The Reader's Digest Association, Inc.
of Pleasantville, New York, U.S.A.

Phototypeset by Tradespools Limited
Frome, Somerset
Printed in Hong Kong
40.133.5

ACKNOWLEDGEMENTS

The publisher would like to thank Caroline Heaton for her help in the compilation of this anthology.

The editor and publisher wish to thank the following for permission to use copyright material in this collection:

Pitman Books Ltd. for 'I had a little cherry stone' by Boyce and Bartlett from *Nursery Rhymes and Finger Plays*; Lesley Churchman for 'The Cuckoo' and 'The Millipede'; Mrs John Drinkwater for 'Snail' and 'Tom-tit' by John Drinkwater; Aileen Fisher for 'Moles' from *Cricket in a Thicket* published by Scribner's, N.Y., 1963; 'Buzzy Old Bees' and

A story of pond life

# The tale of fergus frog

Written by Ruth Thomson
Illustrated by Martin Ursell

PUBLISHED BY THE READER'S DIGEST ASSOCIATION LIMITED

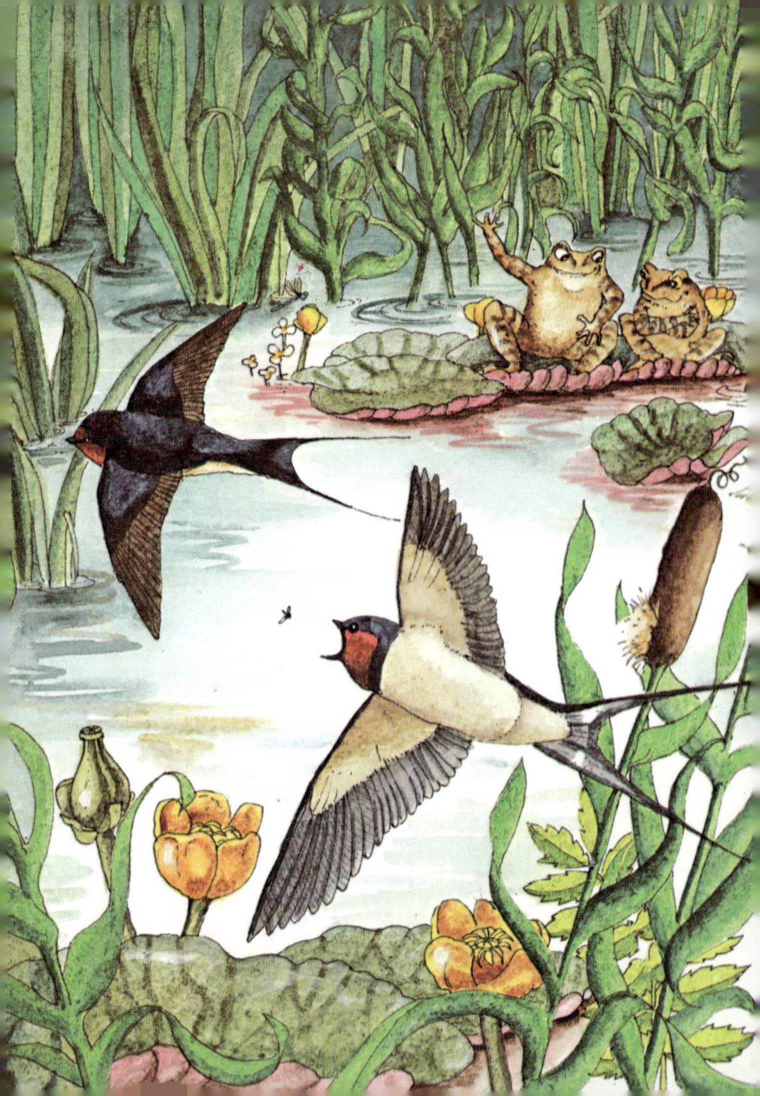

Summer was almost over.
High above the pond,
the swallows were gathering
for their flight to the sun.

Fergus and Bessie sat on a lily pad
watching the swallows
and making the most of the sunshine.
"Hasn't time gone quickly?"
said Fergus. "I can remember
when we were only tadpoles."
"I can remember," said Bessie,
"the very day we hatched."
"A likely story," croaked Fergus.

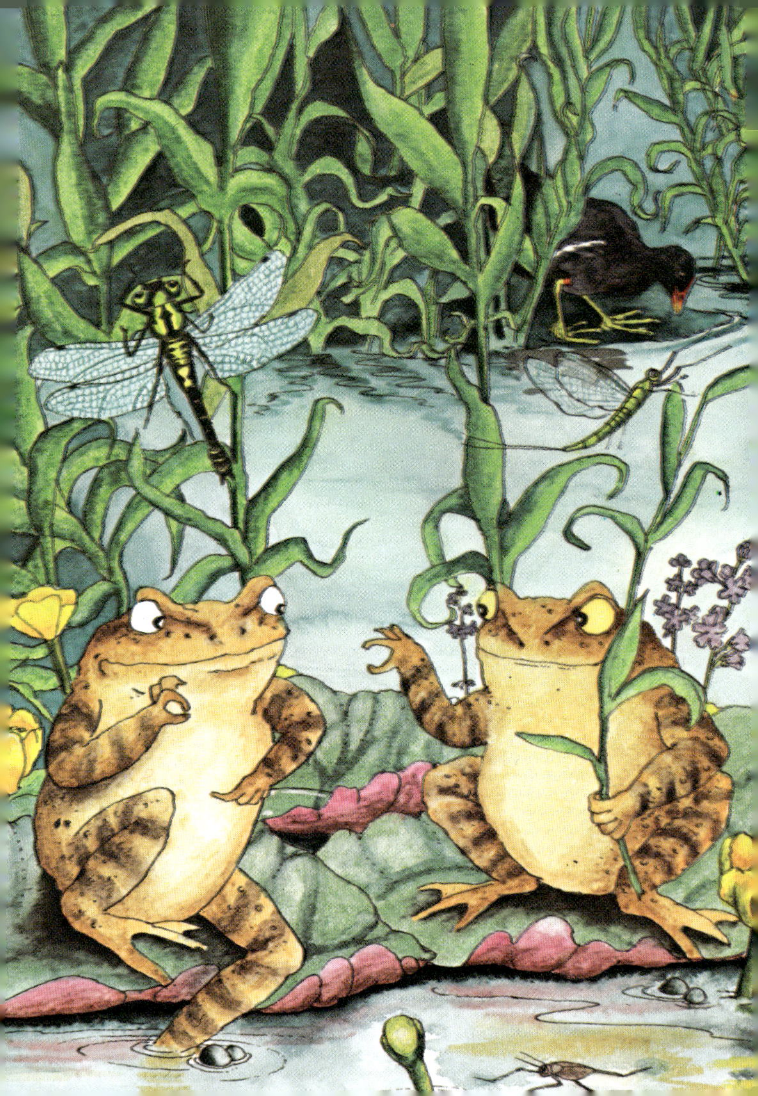

"I can, I can," said Bessie.
"There were thousands of us.
The day we hatched,
the pond was black with tadpoles.

I can remember clinging
to some water-weed
and looking around.
The pond seemed enormous."

"There was so much to see," said Fergus. "I spent days and days wriggling about exploring the pond."
"So did I," said Bessie, "and whenever I felt hungry, I nibbled at some water-weed.

But not everyone was friendly.
I was always on the look-out
for hungry beetles and fish."
"We were lucky to escape,"
agreed Fergus.

"Wasn't it fun to grow so fast," said Bessie, quickly changing the subject.

"Bigger,

and bigger,

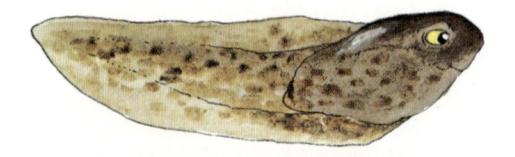

and bigger every day."

"It was even more amazing
to grow legs," interrupted Fergus.

"First back ones,

then front ones."

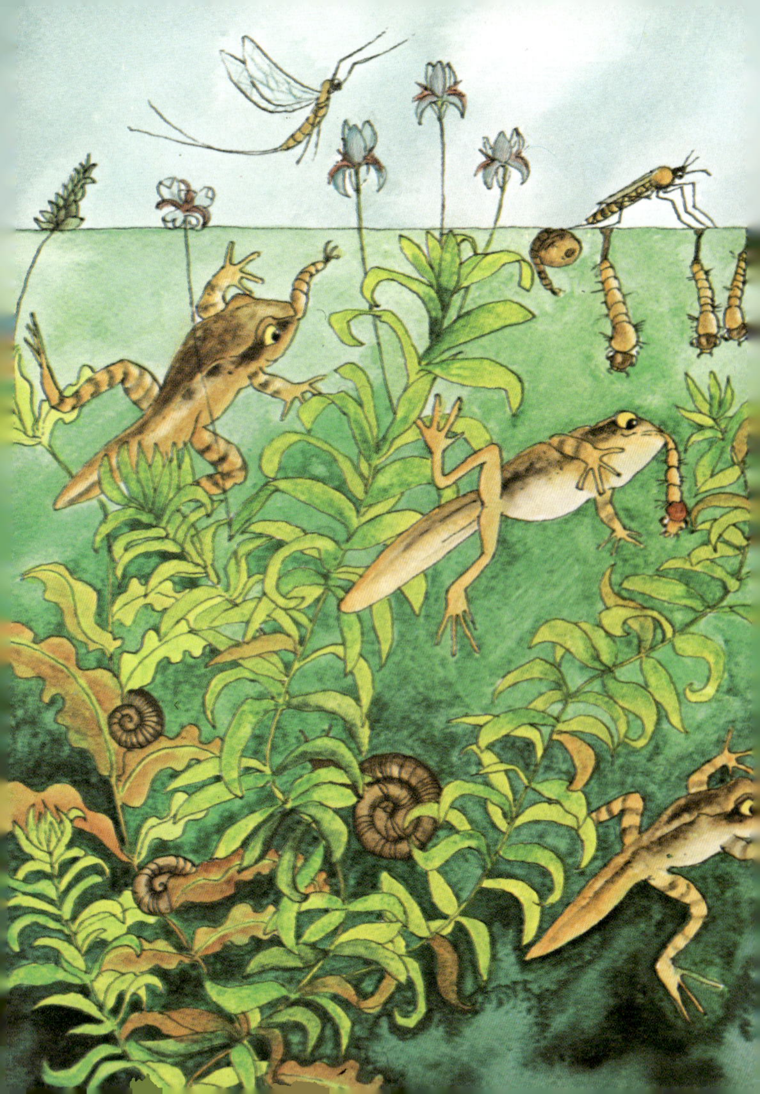

"I liked my new strong jaws as well," said Fergus.

"Me too," replied Bessie, remembering lovely meals of worms and grubs.

"I was sorry to lose my tail in the end," said Fergus.
"You didn't need it anymore, silly," laughed Bessie.
"Not once you were a frog."

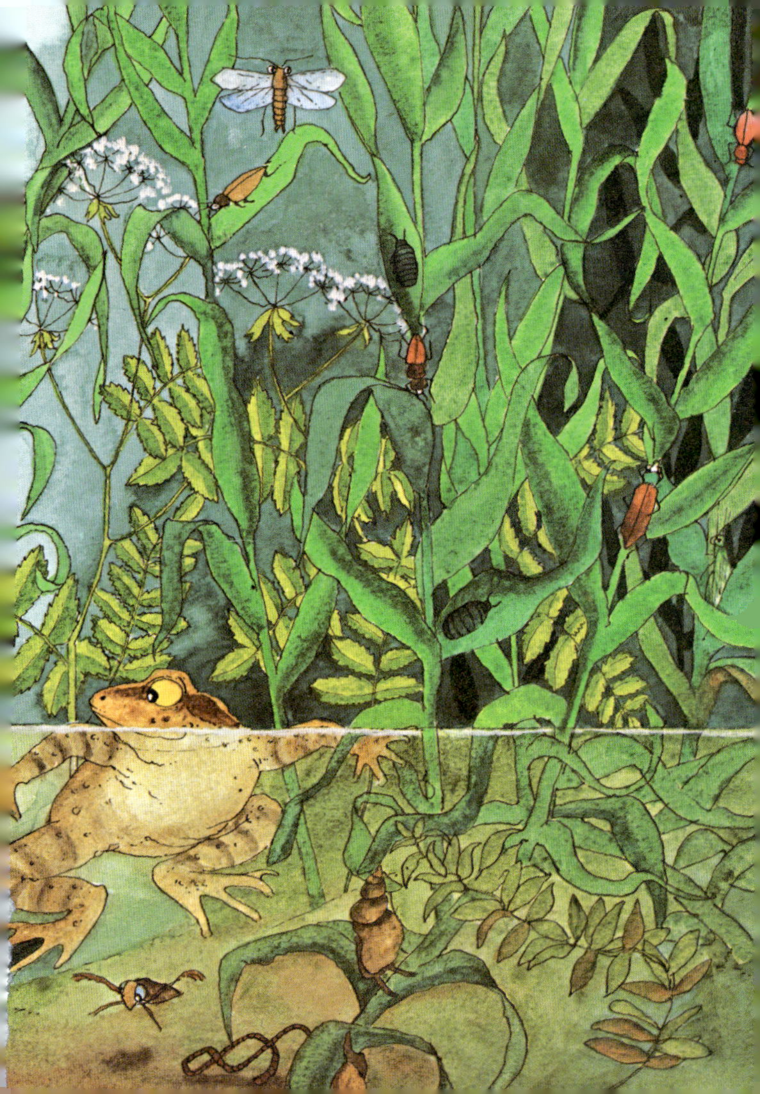

"Do you remember the first time you hopped on to dry land?"
"I certainly do," said Fergus.
"I jumped right into a clump of marsh marigolds."

"That's nothing," said Bessie,
"I jumped right over the rushes."

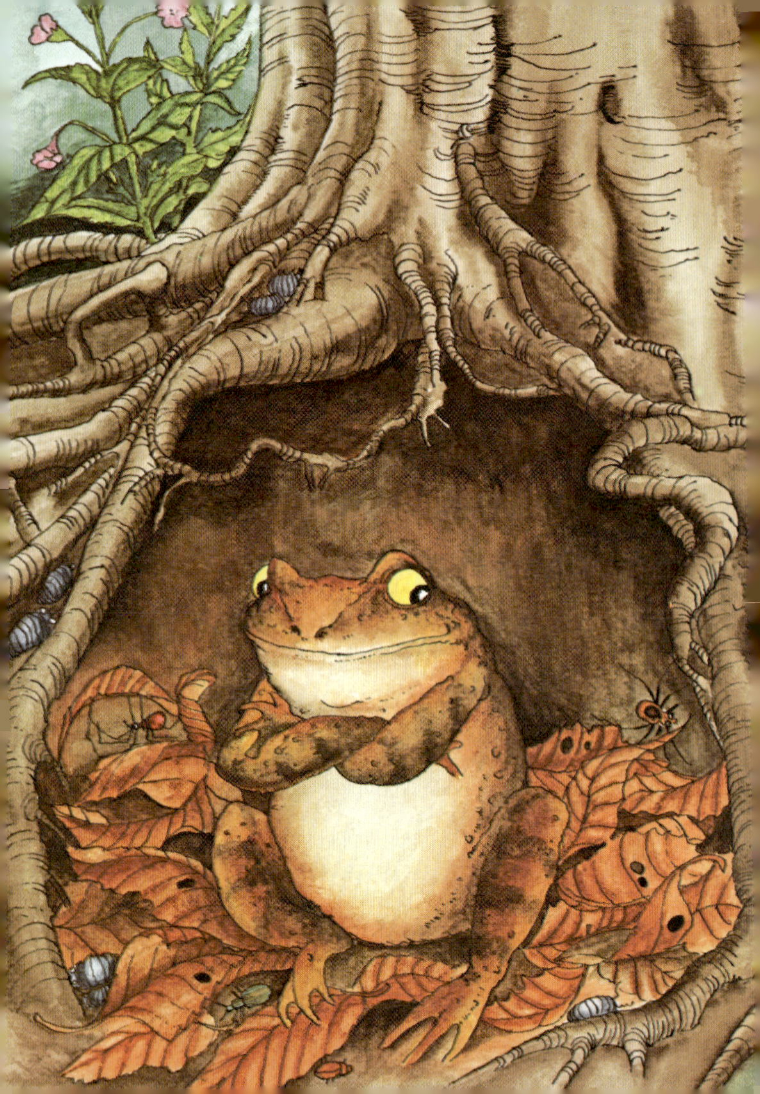

"I found a wonderful place to live," Fergus went on, "among some damp, smelly leaves under a tree."

"I found a better place than that," said Bessie, "under a smooth stone hidden by the reeds."

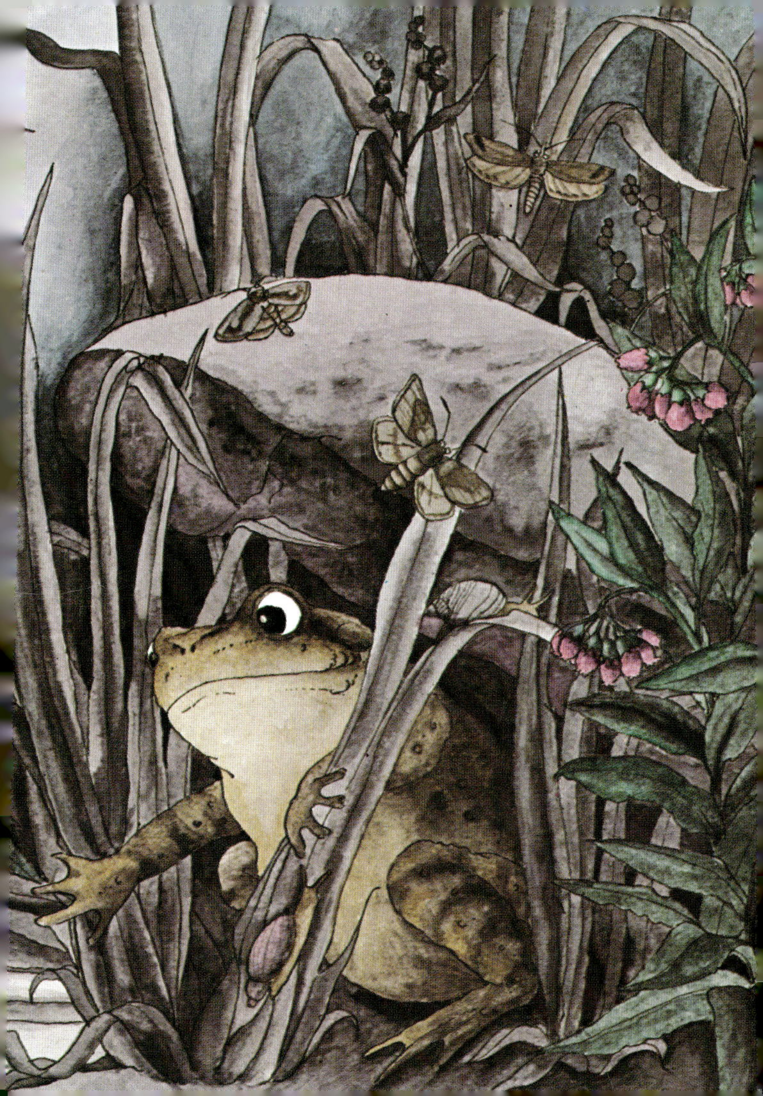

Bessie was beginning to annoy
Fergus. She was so boastful.
"I'll show her," he muttered.
He took a deep breath.
"Do you know," Fergus began,
"that once I sat under my tree
all day and caught
a wriggly worm...

two slimy slugs,

three slow snails,

four juicy caterpillars,

five green grasshoppers,

ten fat beetles,

and two dozen flies?"

"That's nothing," said Bessie,
"Why, I sat on my stone one day
and caught a darting damselfly . . .

two black spiders,

three busy bumblebees,

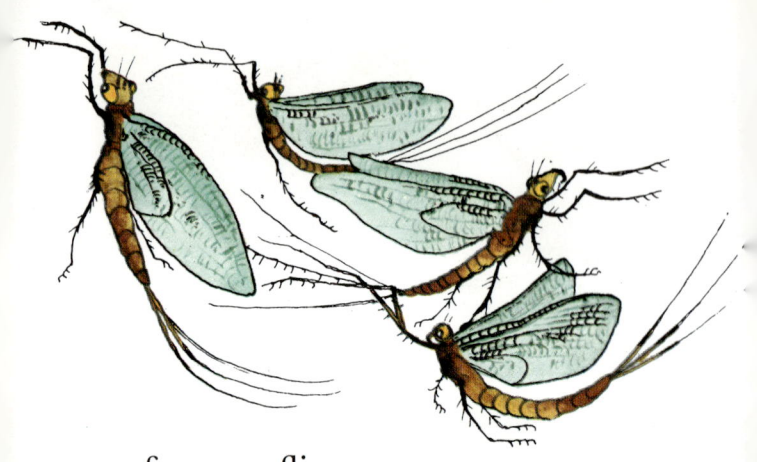

four mayflies,

five beautiful butterflies,

*twenty* fat beetles

and *three dozen* flies!"

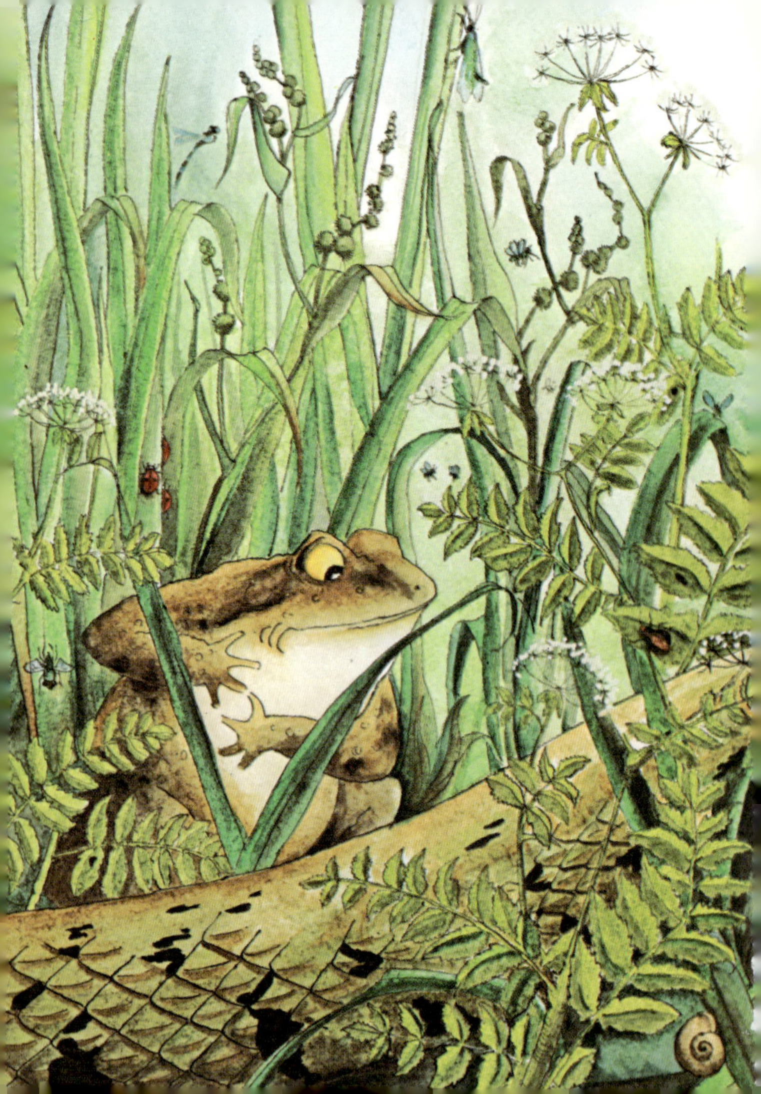

"Do you know," said Fergus quickly,
not to be outdone,
"I had three narrow escapes
all in a row.
One morning a sneaky grass snake
slithered right past my nose.

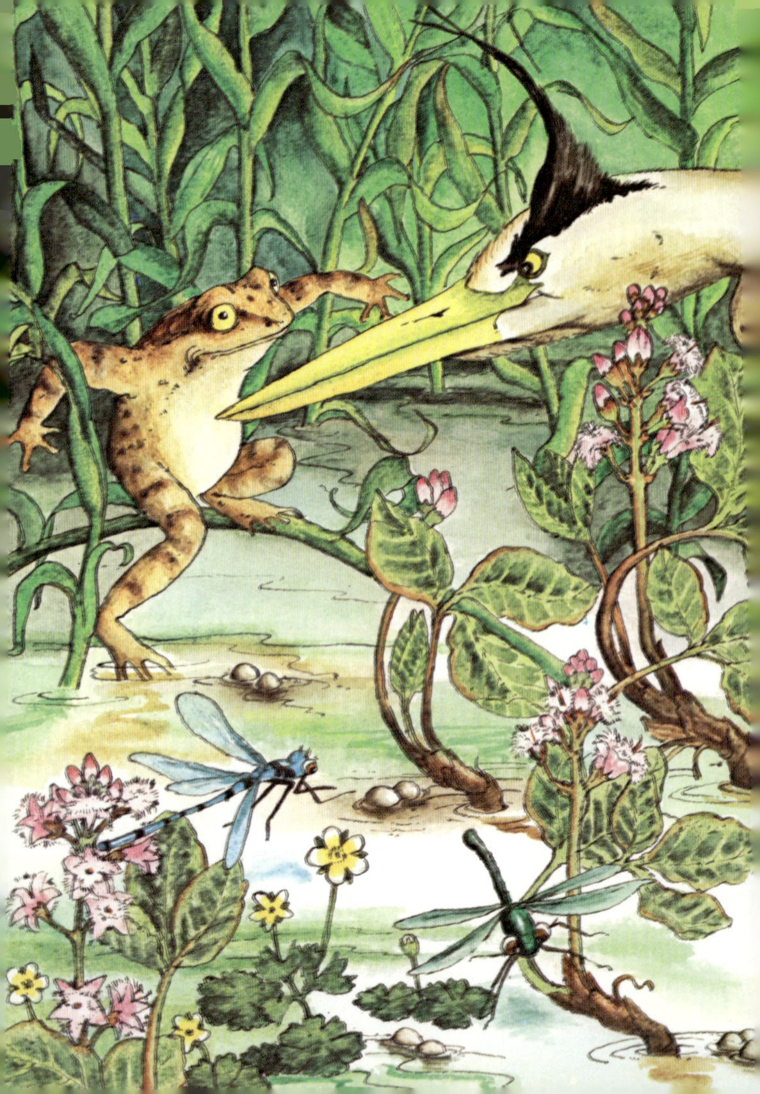

The next day,
a sharp-eyed heron
made a grab for me.

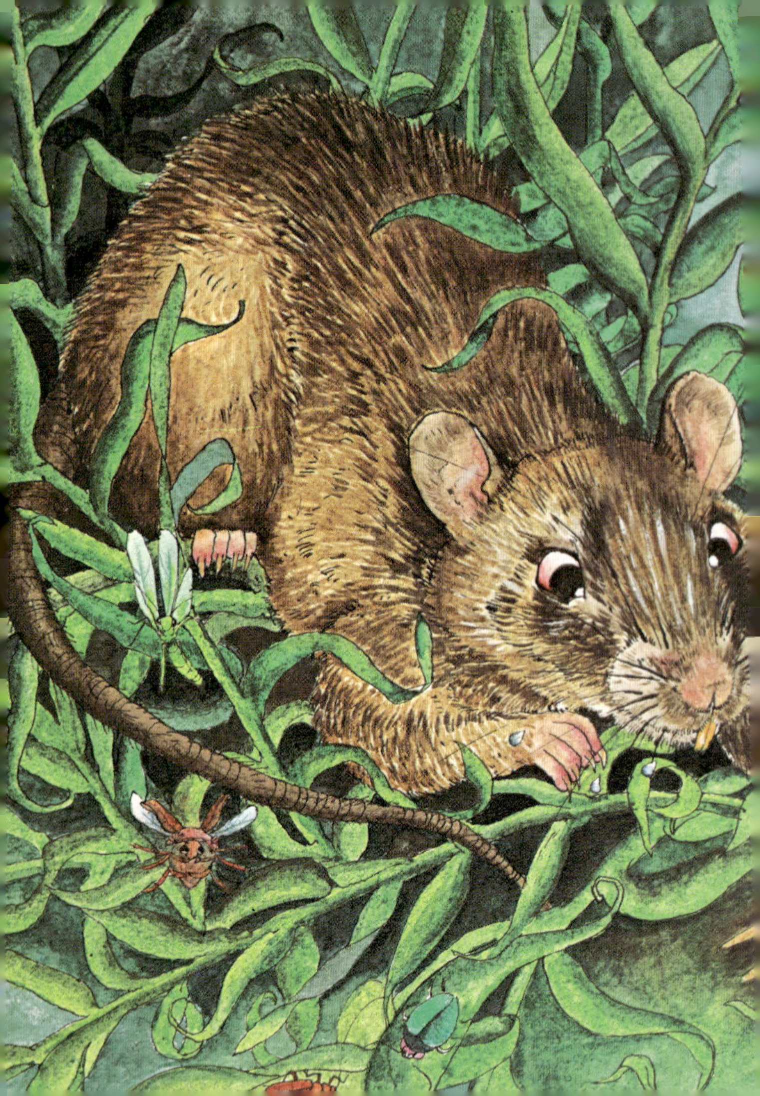

The day after that,
I had to make a quick getaway
from a big brown rat."

"Pooh, pooh," said Bessie,
"That's nothing at all.
I had three narrow escapes
all in one evening.

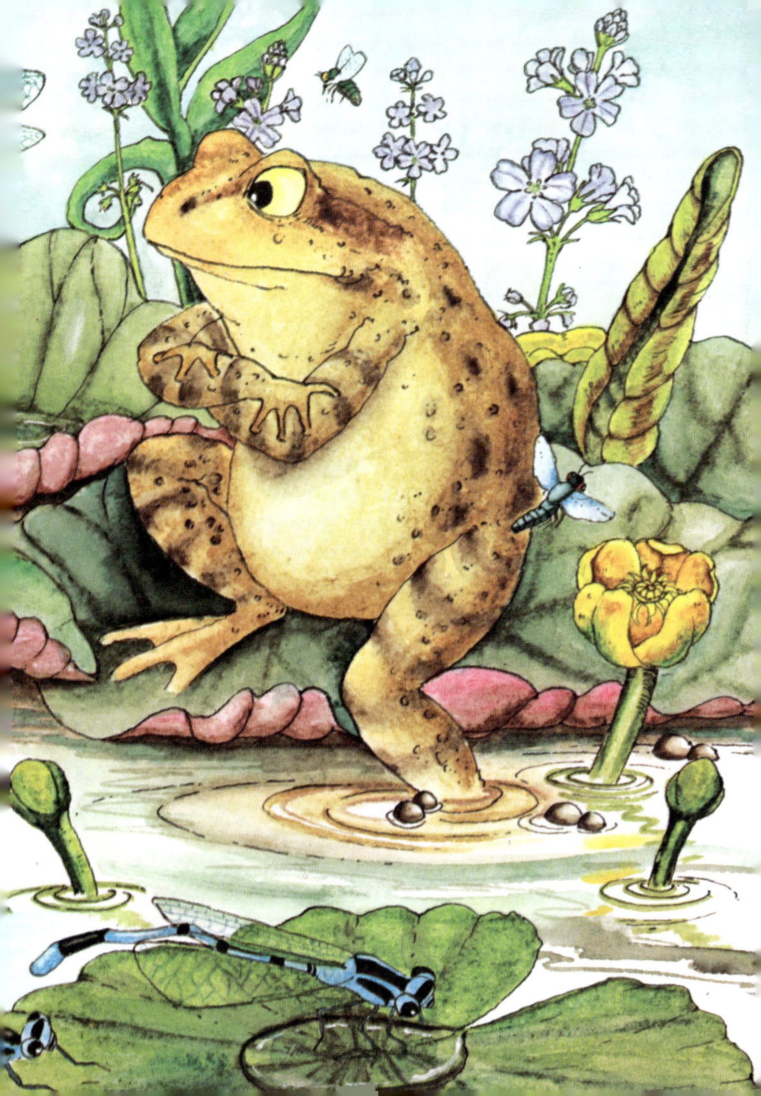

"First of all,
an enormous owl came swooping
down from the sky.
I dived into the pond to escape
and came face to face with . . .

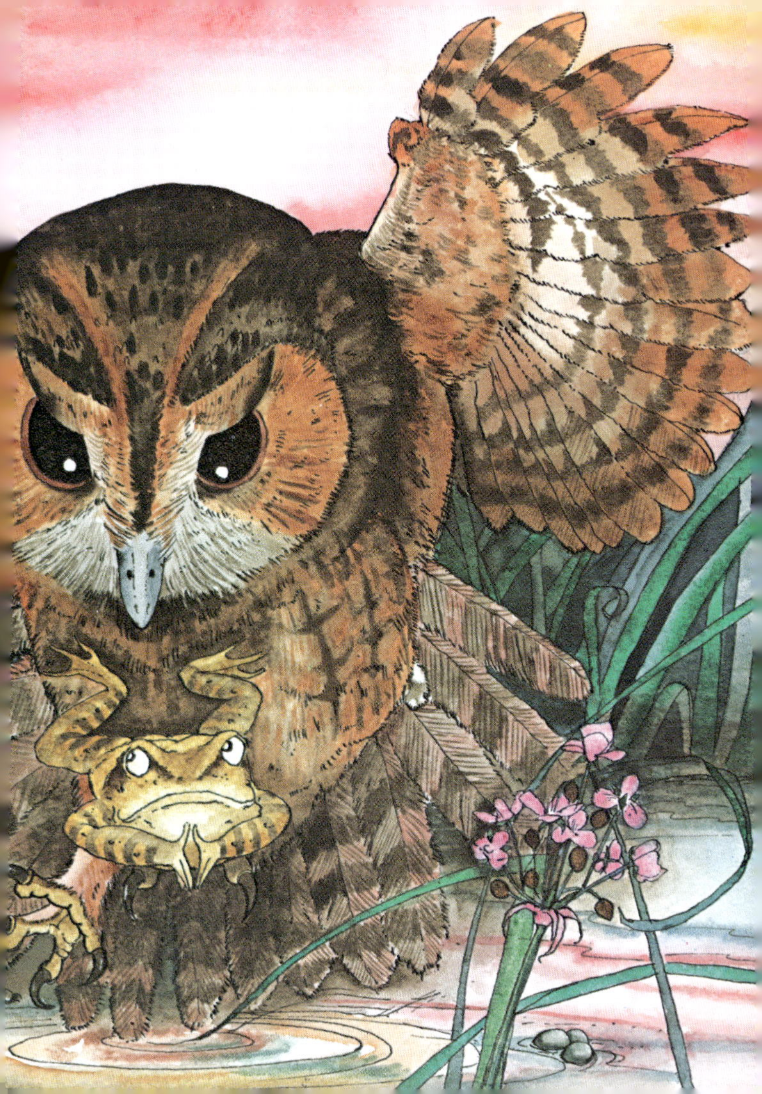

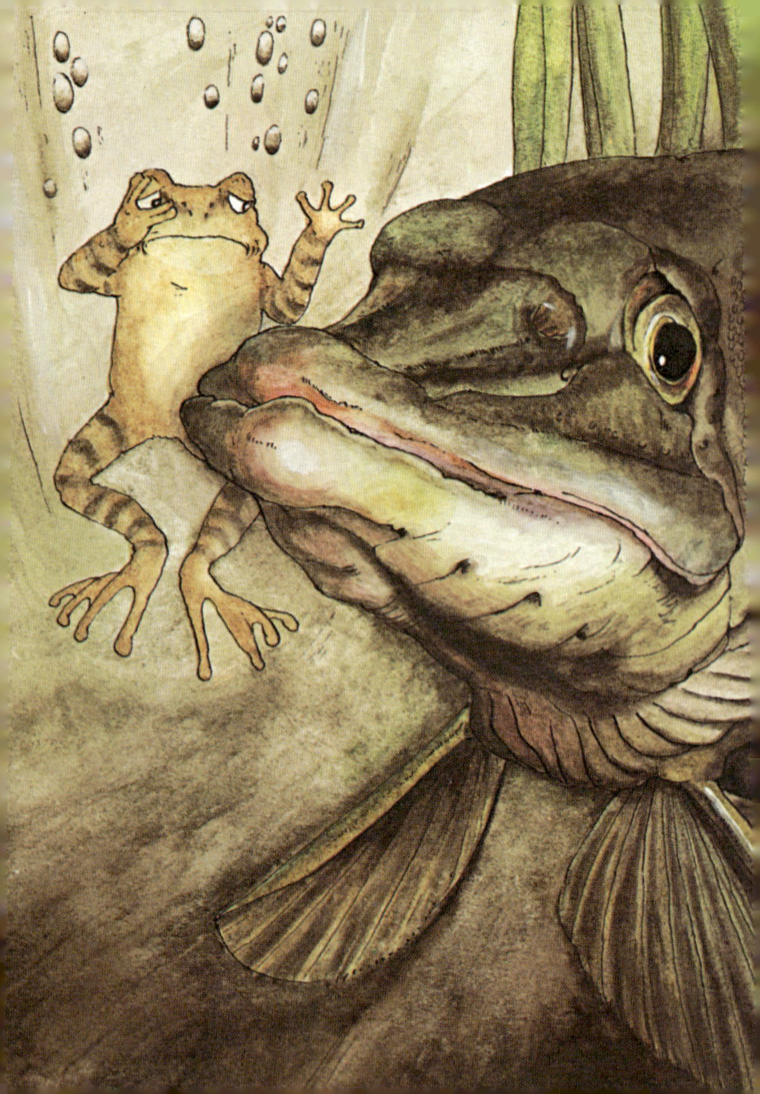

a fearsome pike
lurking in the reeds.
I leaped back on the shore
and almost bumped into . . .

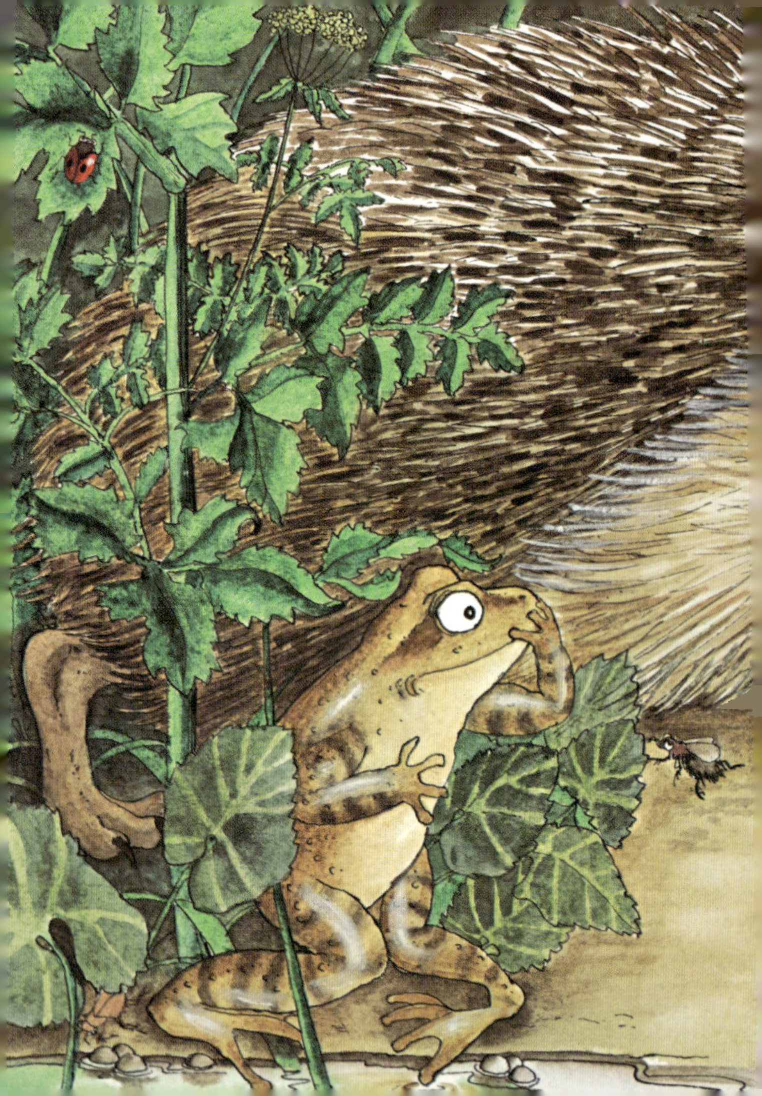

a hungry hedgehog
snuffling around for food.
I was quite worn out
after that, I can tell you."

Fergus didn't know
quite what to say.
He thought quickly.
"Do you know," he said,
"that whenever there's a rainstorm
I come out and leap
higher than the grass?"

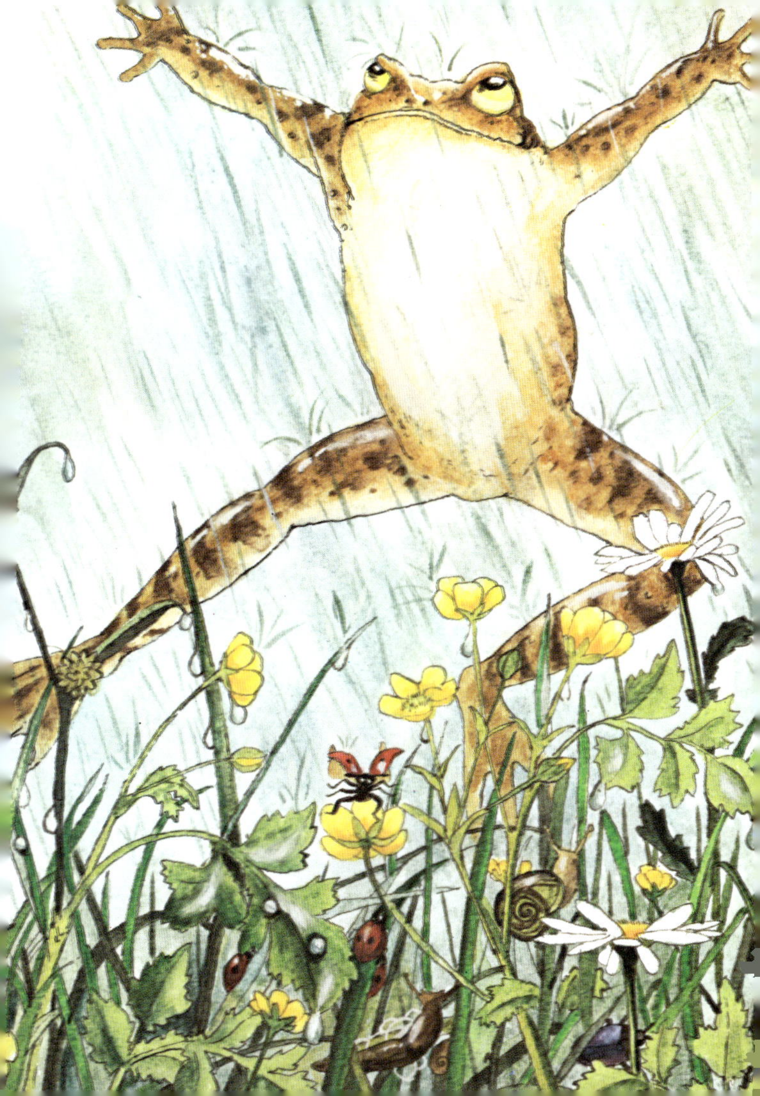

"That's nothing," said Bessie,
I've leaped higher than the moon."
Fergus knew that couldn't be true,
but he didn't say anything.

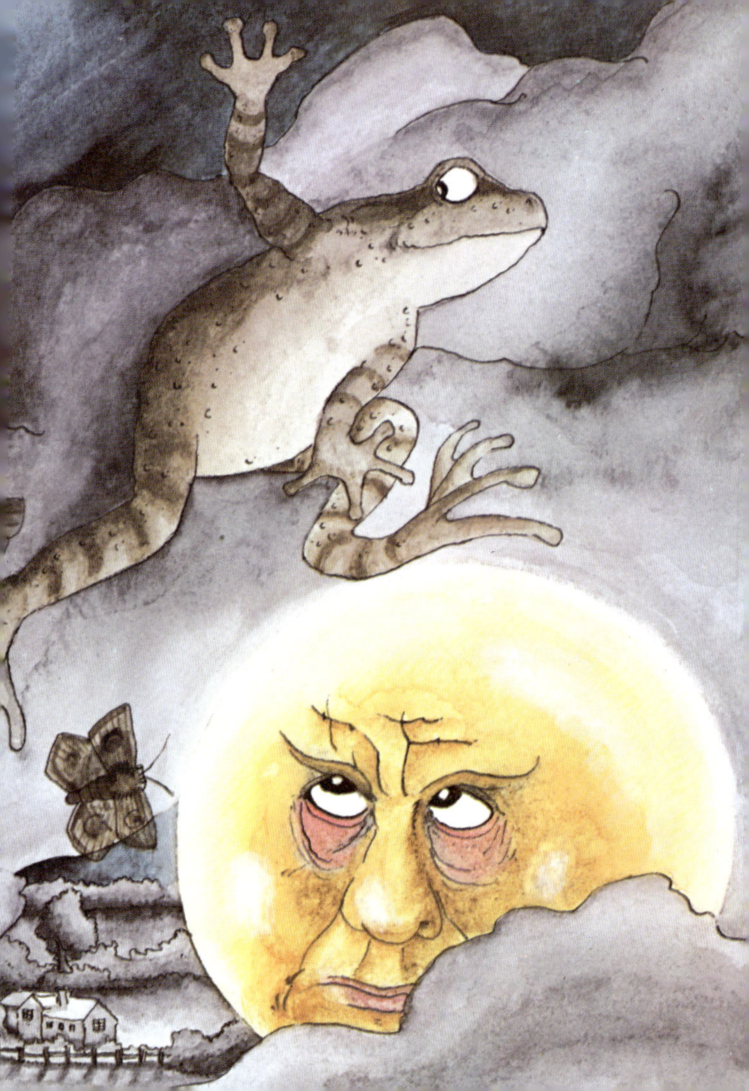

After a long silence, Fergus said,
"I've found a wonderful hole
to sleep in for the winter."
Bessie turned to look at him.

"Yes," said Fergus smugly.
"When the wind blows
and the pond freezes
and the snow falls, I'll be warm
and cosy."

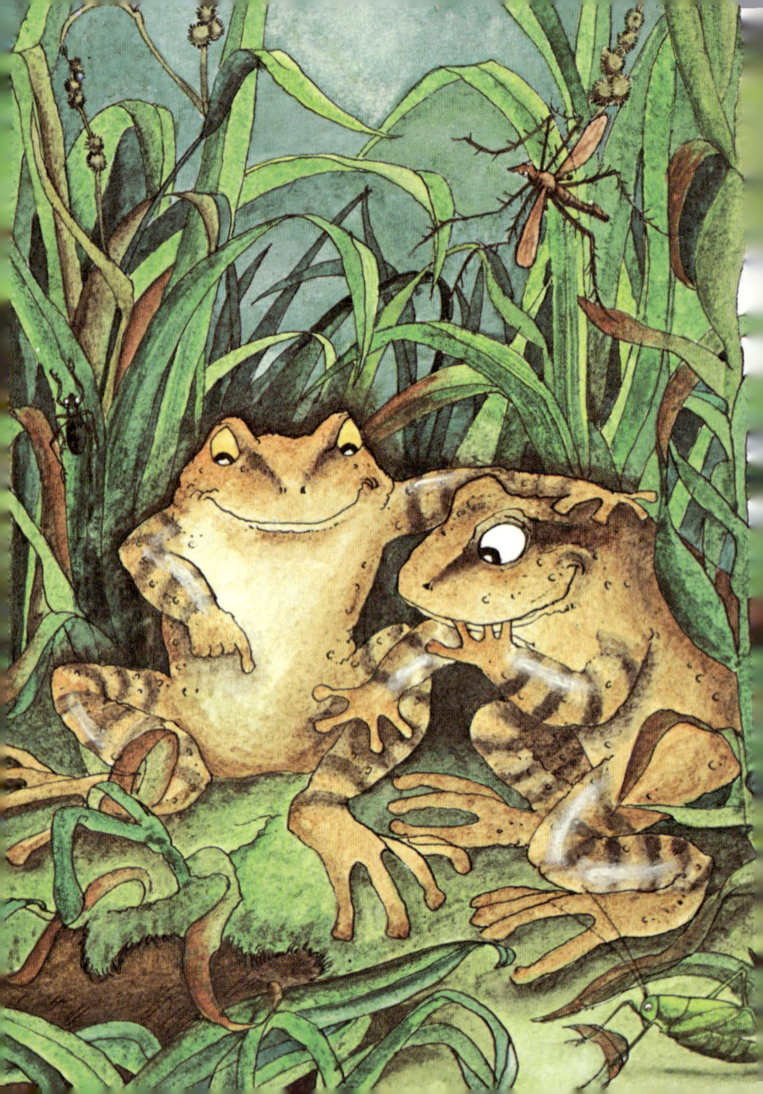

Bessie hadn't found a hole.
She thought about what Fergus said
and gave a shiver.
In a small voice, she said,
"Do you think I could share it
with you?"
"Of course," said Fergus,
feeling extra pleased with himself.
"Come and have a look at it."
Bessie thought it was
a splendid hole.

When the days started
getting shorter,
the two frogs crept into the hole
and huddled together.
Outside, a cold wind blew.
The leaves fell off the trees
and the sun scarcely shone.

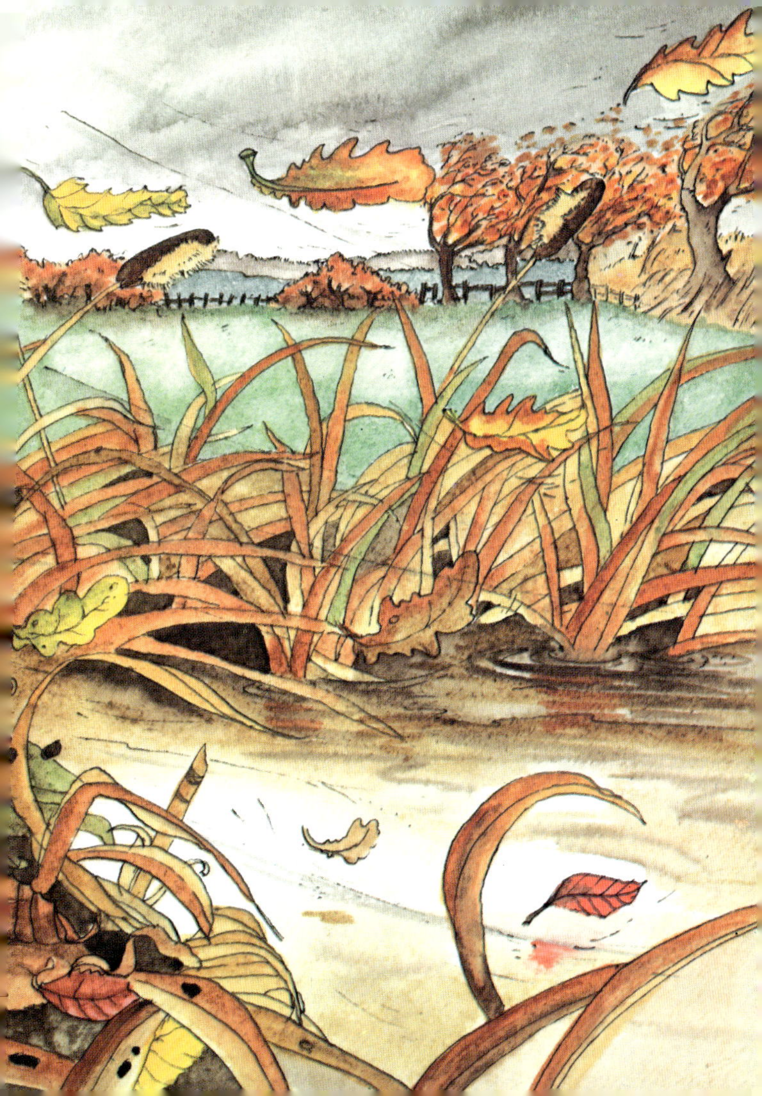

Winter came.
Snow fell on the fields
and the ditches.
The pond froze.
Hungry ducks slithered
over the ice looking for food.

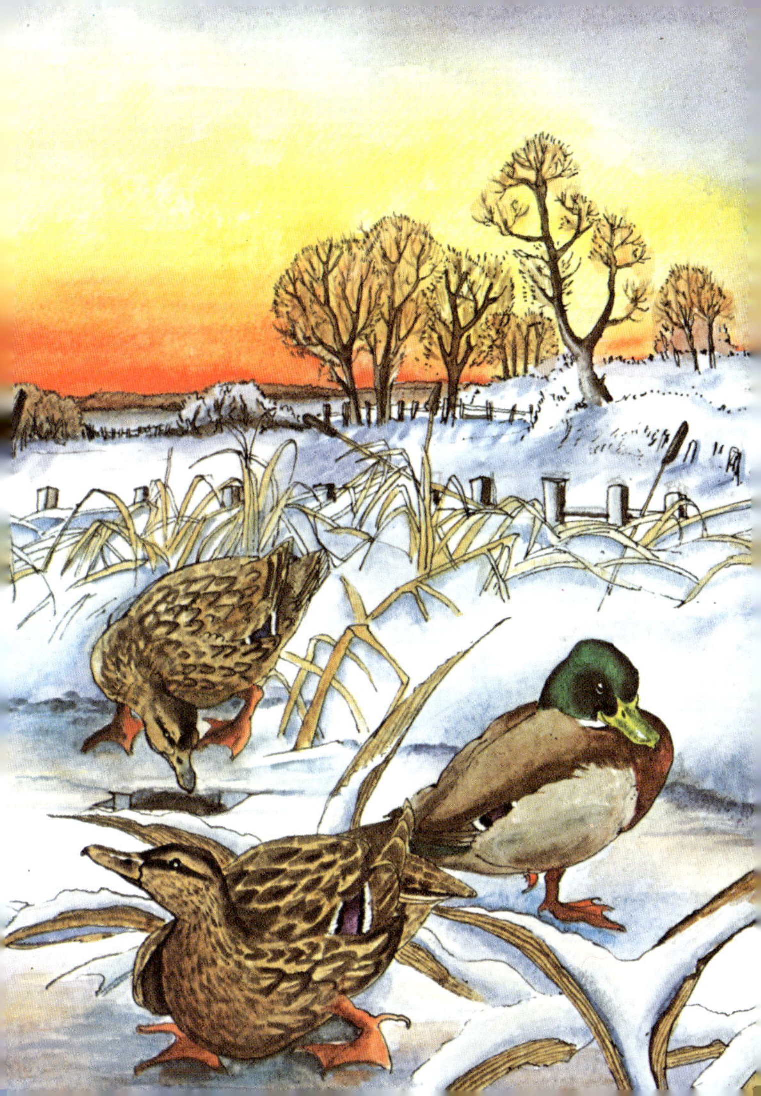

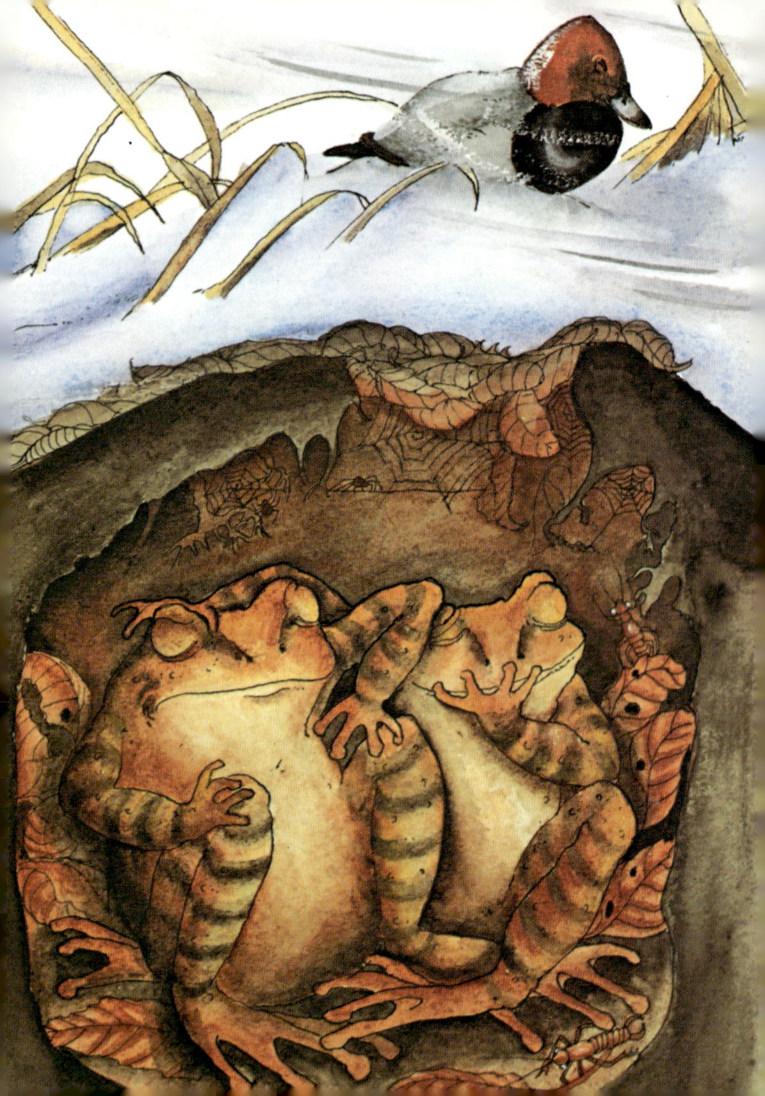

The two frogs slept on and on
in their snug little hole.
They didn't even wake up
for Christmas.

They woke up
only when the snow had melted
and the buds were on the trees.
"See you here next year,"
said Fergus, as he leaped off
to find some food.
"Only if I don't find
a better sort of hole,"
said Bessie leap-frogging over him,
down to the pond.

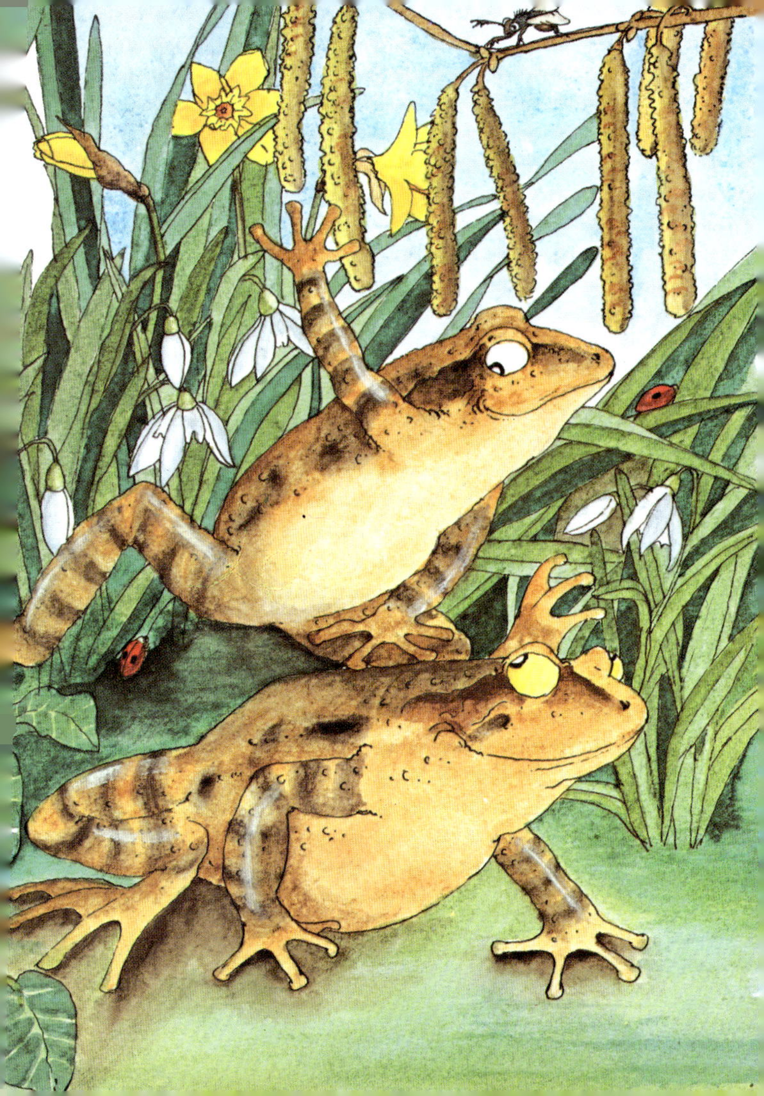

MY NATURE LIBRARY

First Edition Copyright © 1982
The Reader's Digest Association
Limited, Berkeley Square House,
Berkeley Square, London W1X 6AB
Reprinted 1992

All rights reserved

® READER'S DIGEST, THE DIGEST and
the Pegasus logo are registered trademarks of
The Reader's Digest Association, Inc.
of Pleasantville, New York, U.S.A.

Phototypeset by Tradespools Limited
Frome, Somerset
Printed in Hong Kong
40.133.5

A flower story

# A feast of flowers

Written by Ruth Thomson
Illustrated by Gill Tomblin

PUBLISHED BY THE READER'S DIGEST ASSOCIATION LIMITED

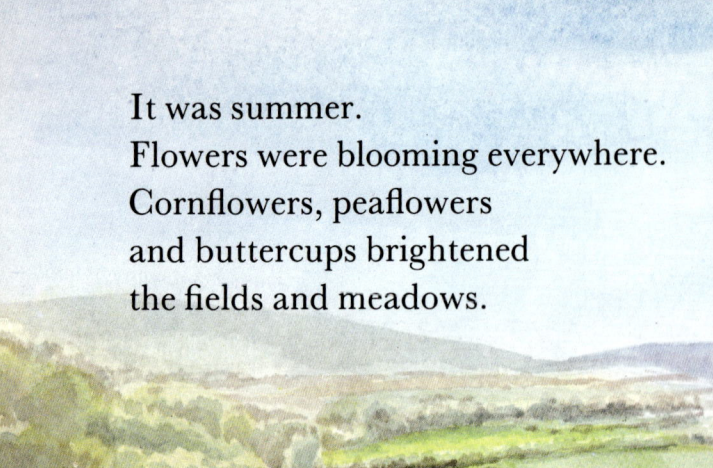

It was summer.
Flowers were blooming everywhere.
Cornflowers, peaflowers
and buttercups brightened
the fields and meadows.

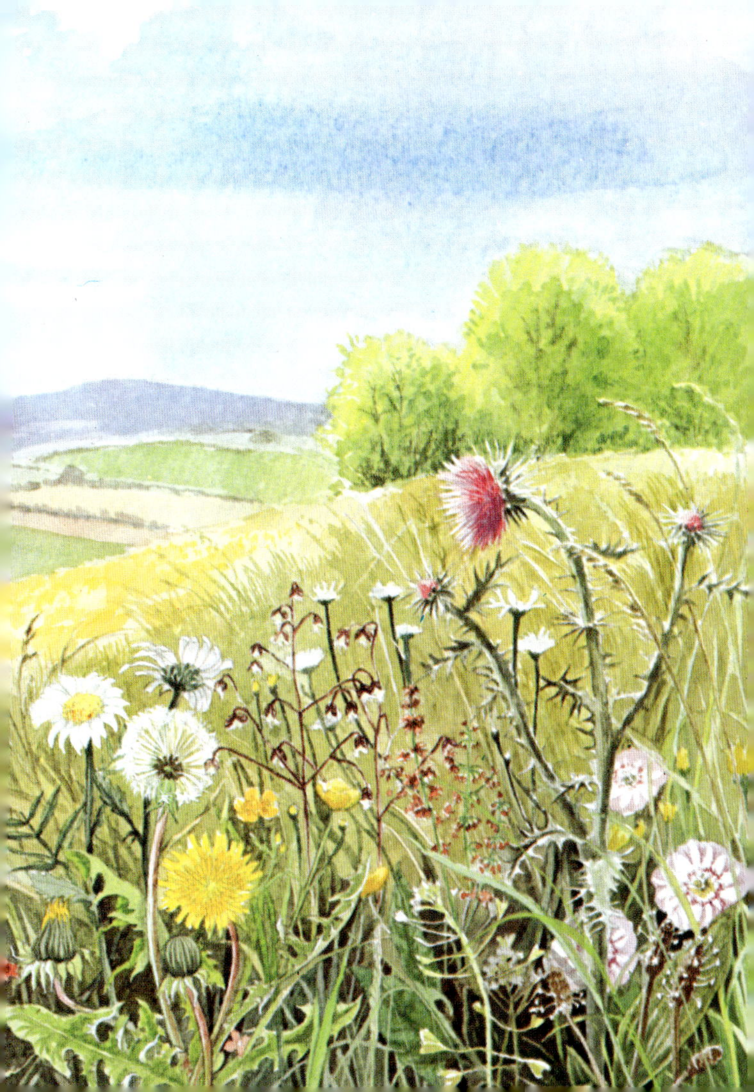

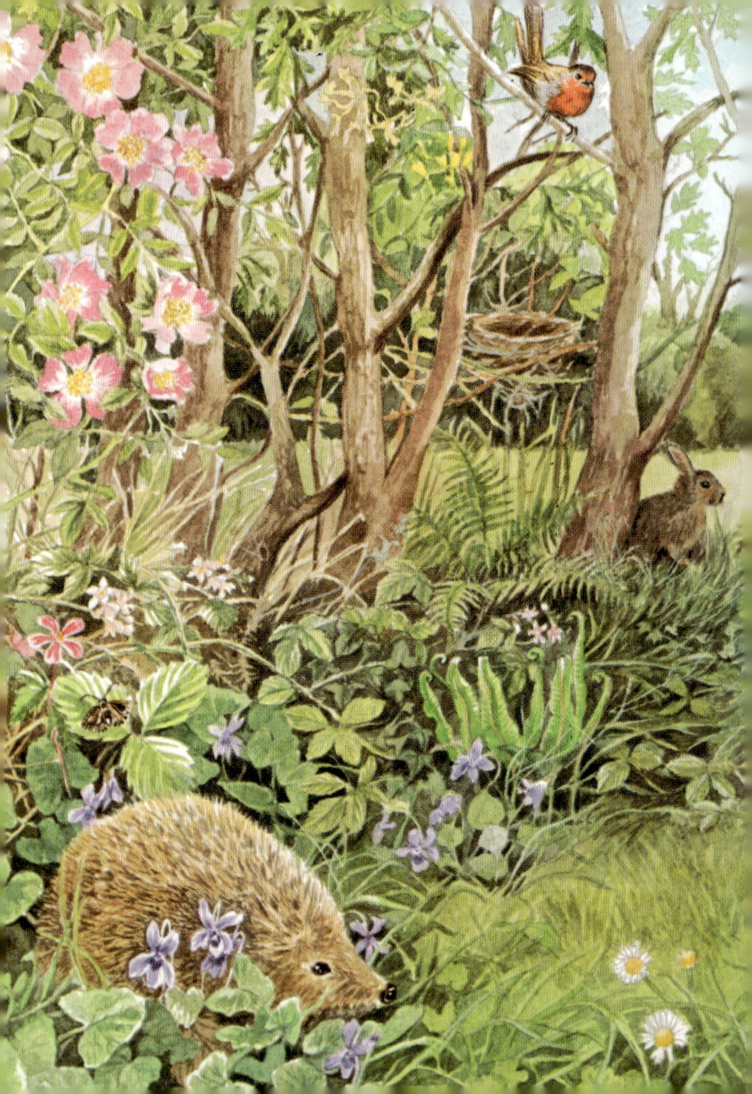

Dog roses and violets cheered the hedges.

Cow parsley and dandelions lined the roadsides and footpaths.

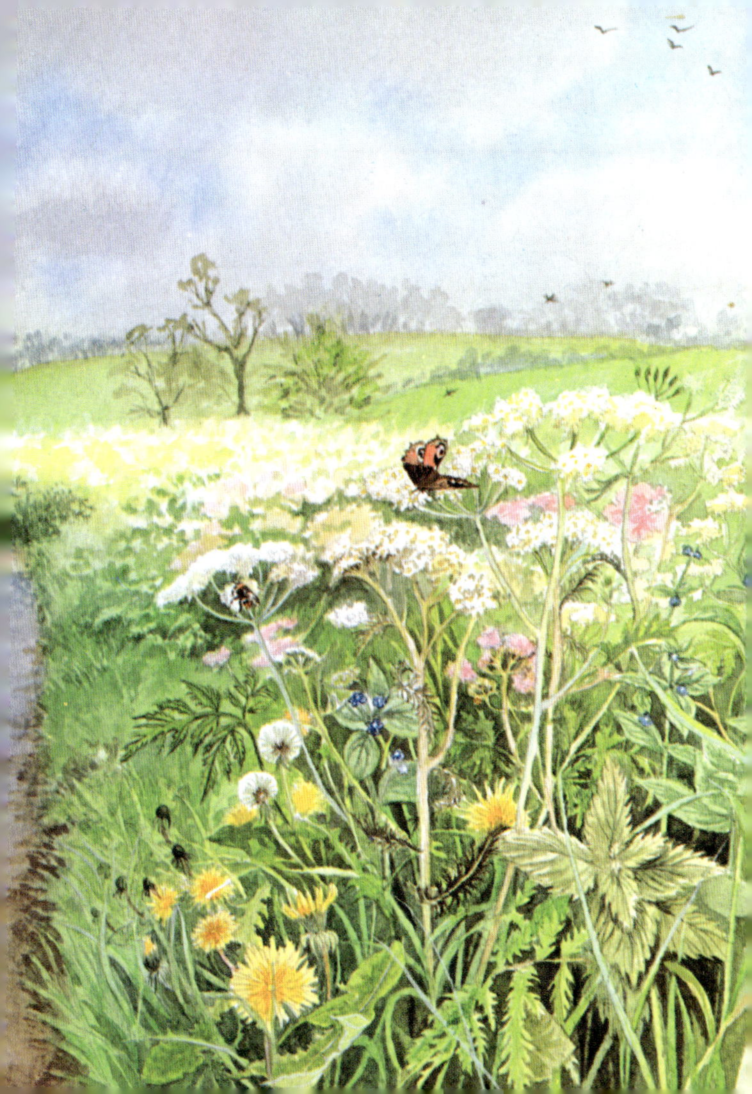

Purple loosestrife and meadowsweet
bloomed along the riverbanks,
and water lilies opened proudly
on the still water of the pond.

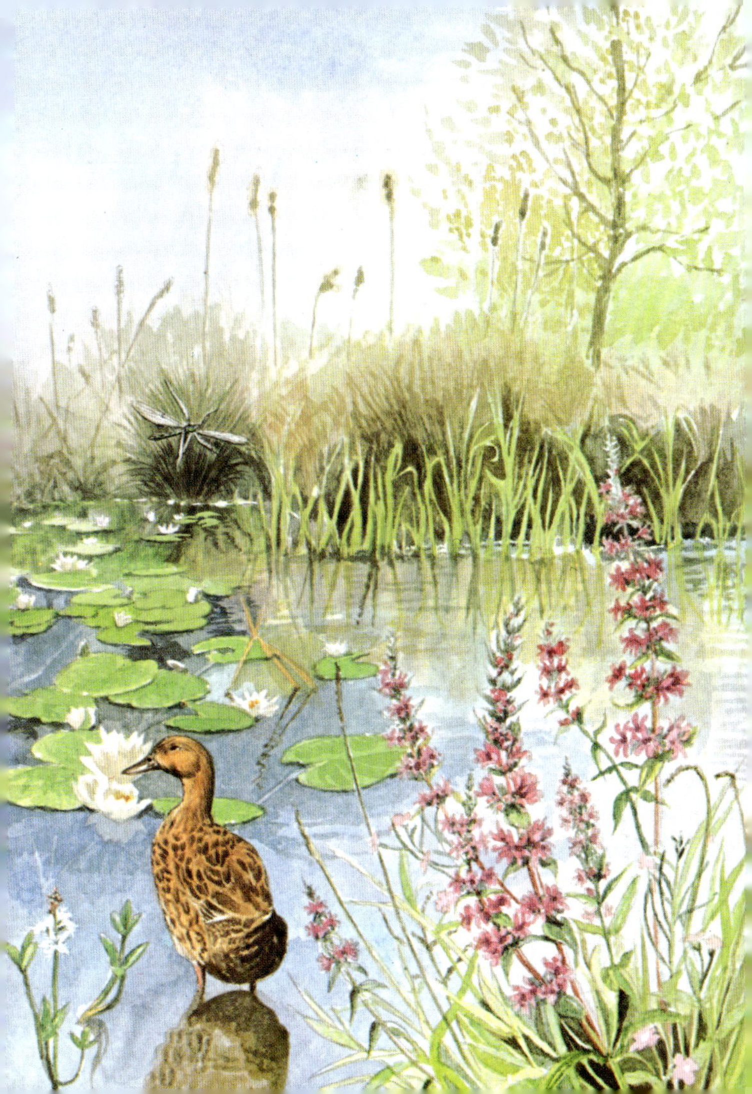

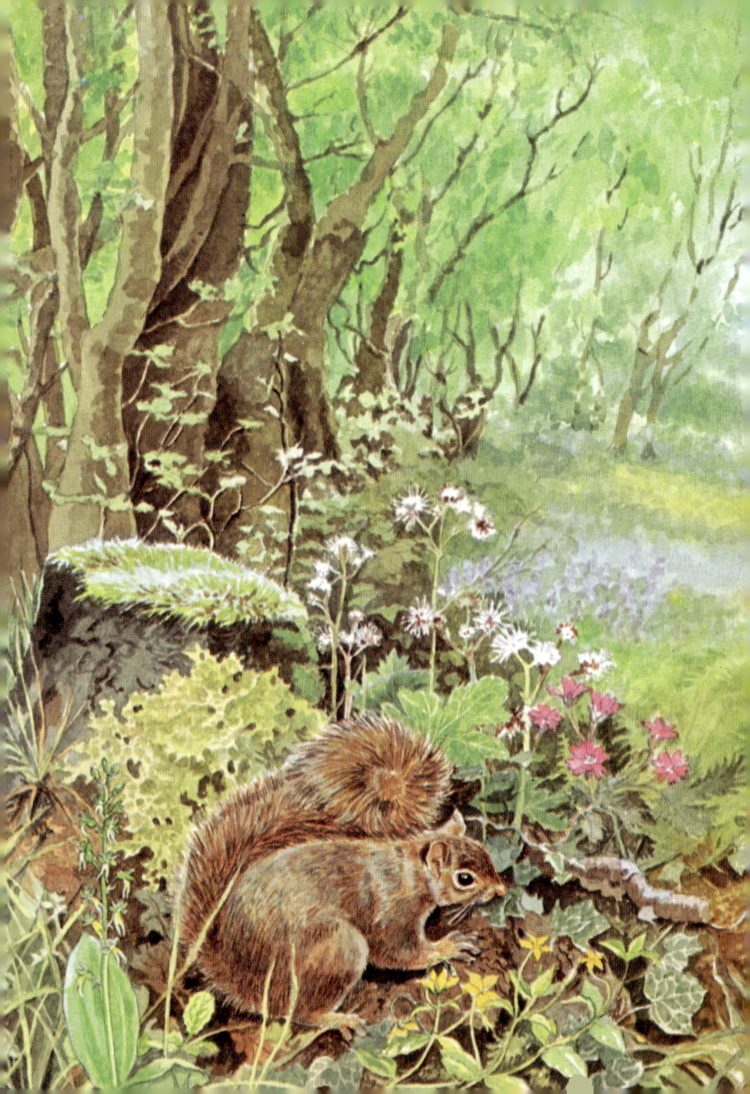

Yellow pimpernels carpeted
the woodland glades.

Crowds of insects
hummed and buzzed
and whizzed and whirred
around all the flowers.

Among these insects was Busybee.

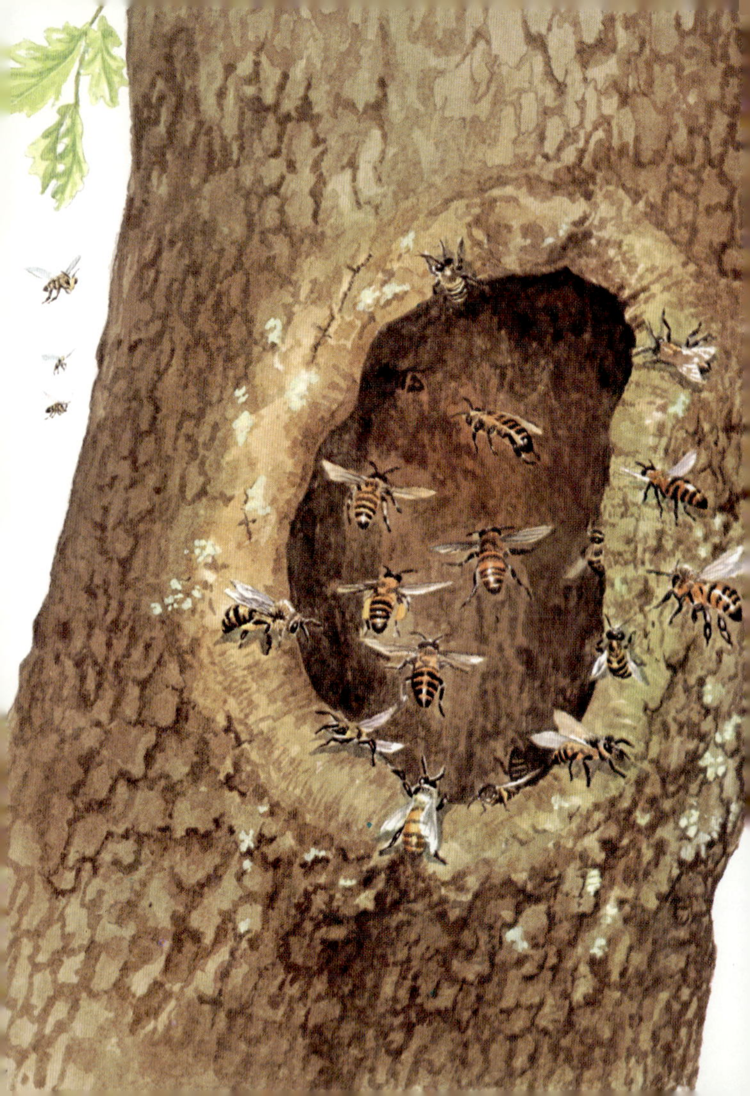

Busybee lived in the hollow
of a tree along with thousands
and thousands of other bees.
The bees were always very busy.

The queen bee was busy
all day long laying eggs.

The youngest bees were busy cleaning out cells for the eggs to go in.

Nurse bees were busy feeding bee grubs with honey and pollen.

Young bees were busy making cells for even more eggs.

Older bees were busy making honey or cleaning out the nest.

The oldest bees of all collected
nectar and pollen from flowers.
Busybee was one of the oldest bees.
She was very proud.
She liked to go out alone
early every morning.
She thought she knew where to find
the best supply of nectar.

One morning, while Busybee was out, her friend, Lizziebee, came flying into the nest in a great hurry.
"I've found some wonderful nectar for us all," she buzzed.
"Tell us where, tell us where," said the bees, crowding excitedly around the entrance to the nest.

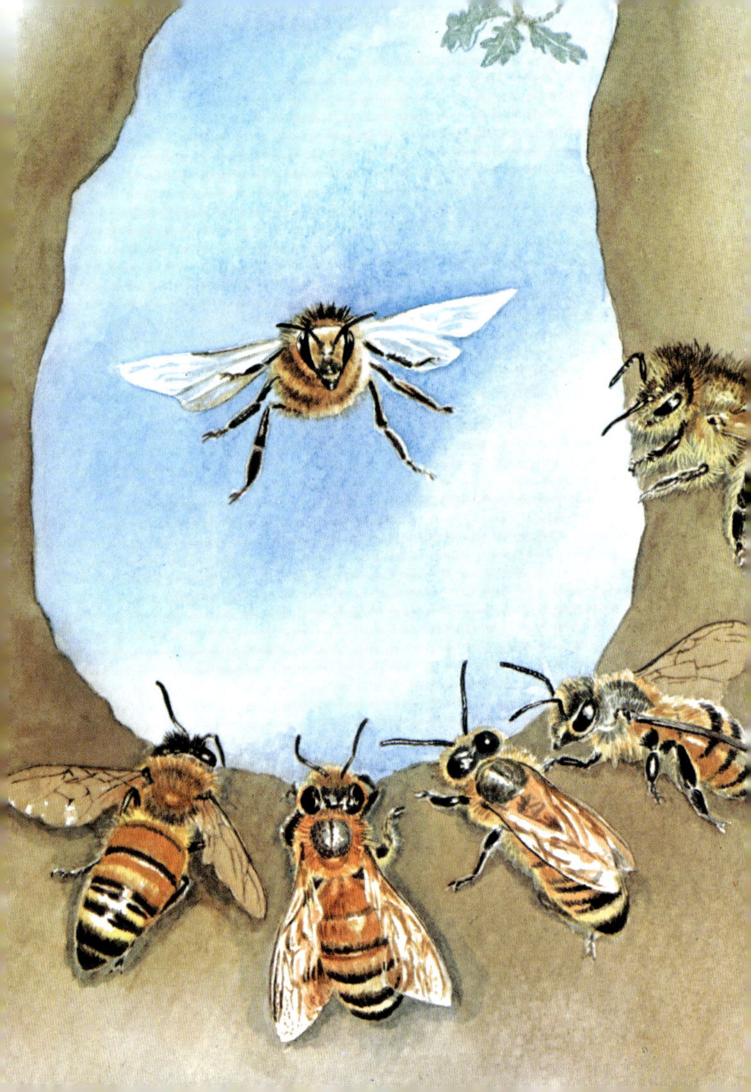

Wiggle, waggle. Wiggle, waggle.
Lizziebee danced round
in a figure of eight and ran
forward to show the direction
of the nectar.

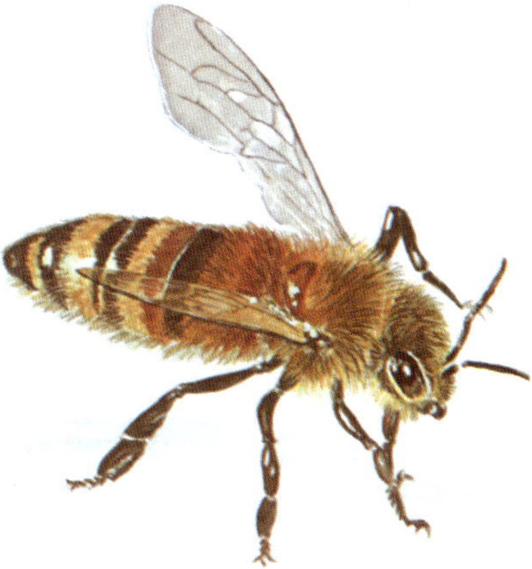

That was enough for the bees.
They zoomed off at once,
anxious not to miss a single drop.

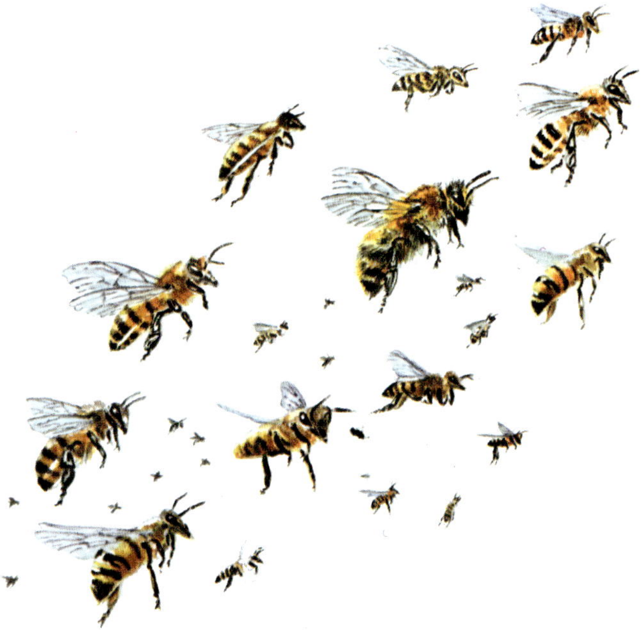

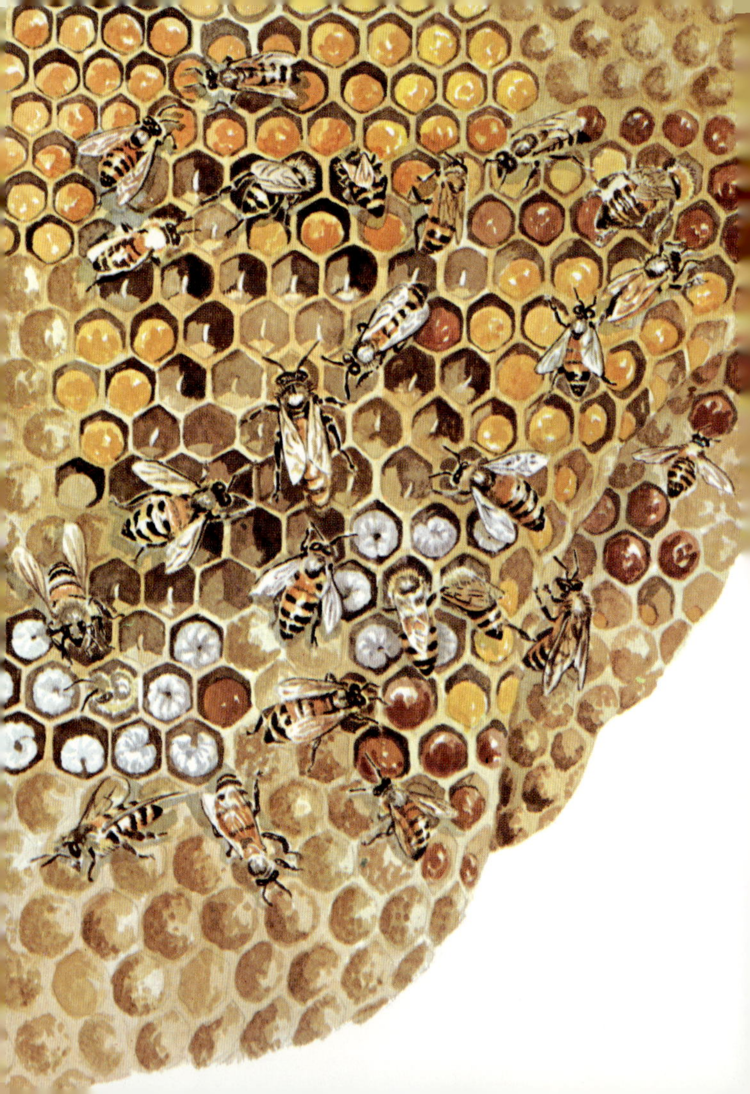

When Busybee returned to the nest,
it was very quiet.
The young bees were all hard
at work, but where were her friends?
"They've gone to find
a wonderful supply of nectar,"
said one of the bees.
"Where?" buzzed Busybee impatiently.
The bee didn't know.
Busybee set off to find them.
She looked everywhere.

They weren't in the foxgloves,

nor among the forget-me-nots.

nor on the cornflowers,

nor on the honeysuckle.
Where could they be?

They weren't on the dog roses.
Some flower beetles were there,
having a feast of pollen.

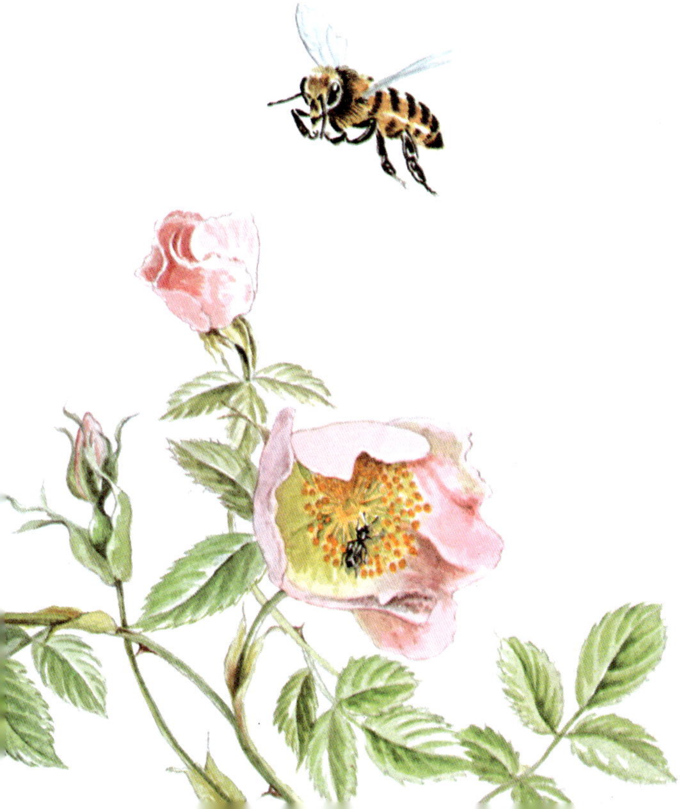

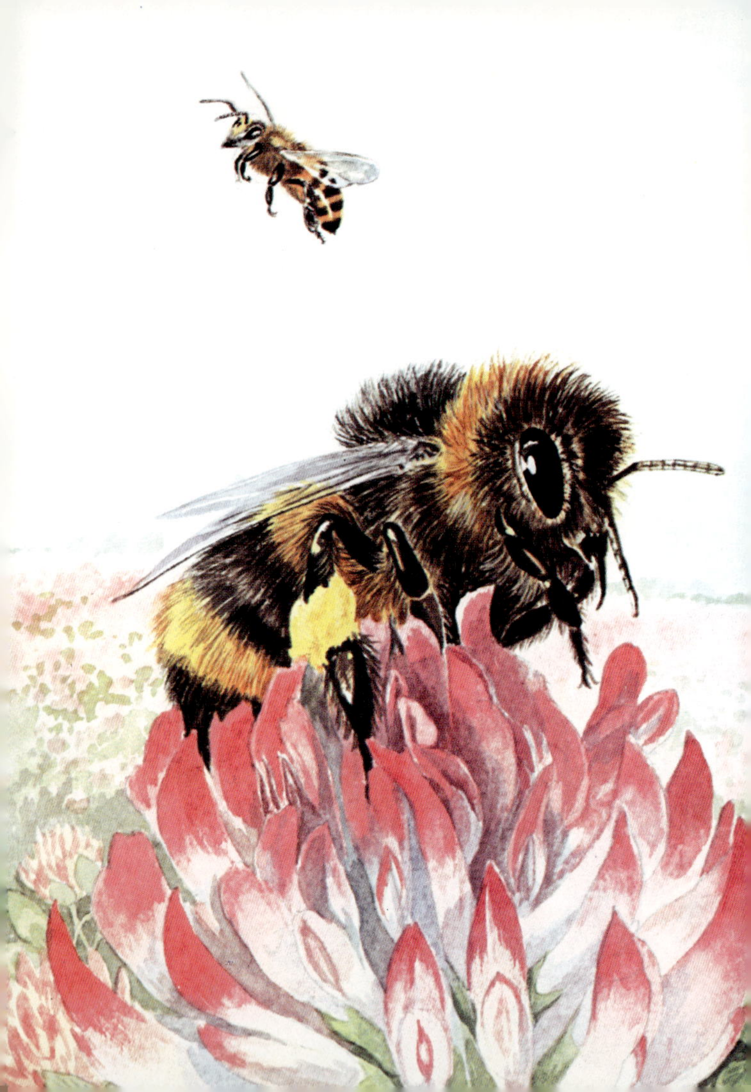

They weren't in the clover field.
That was buzzing with bumblebees.

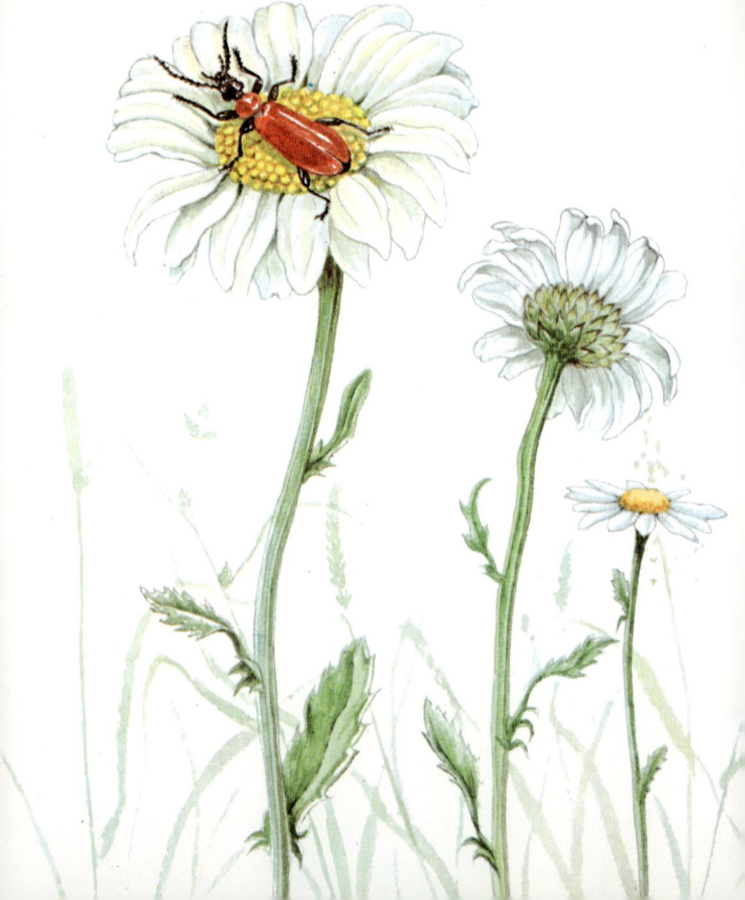

They weren't on the daisies.
A lonely cardinal beetle
was the only insect she saw
on one of those.

"Have you seen the honeybees?" she asked a solitary wasp feeding on cow parsley.
The wasp ignored her.

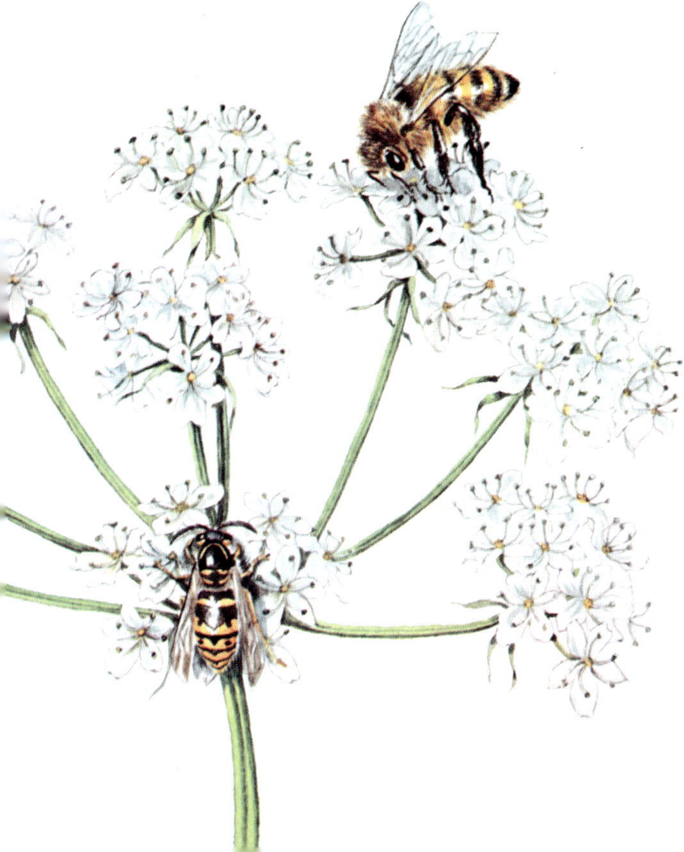

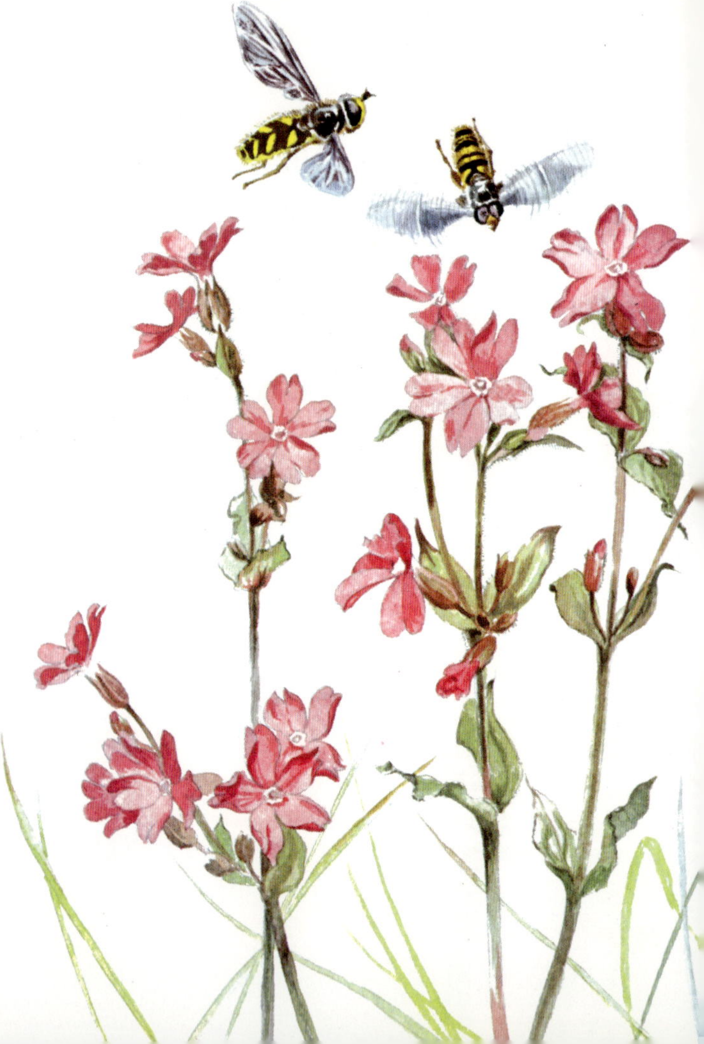

"Have you seen the honeybees?"
she asked two hoverflies
hovering over some red campion.

They shook their heads.

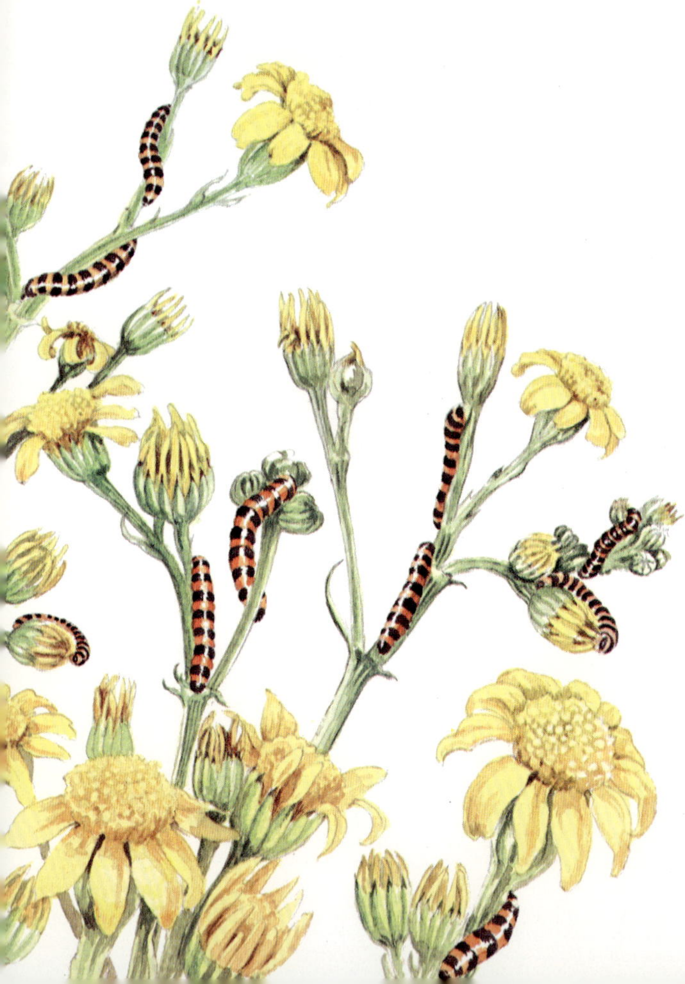

"Have you seen the honeybees?"
she asked the cinnabar
caterpillars climbing up
the ragwort stalks.
They didn't answer.

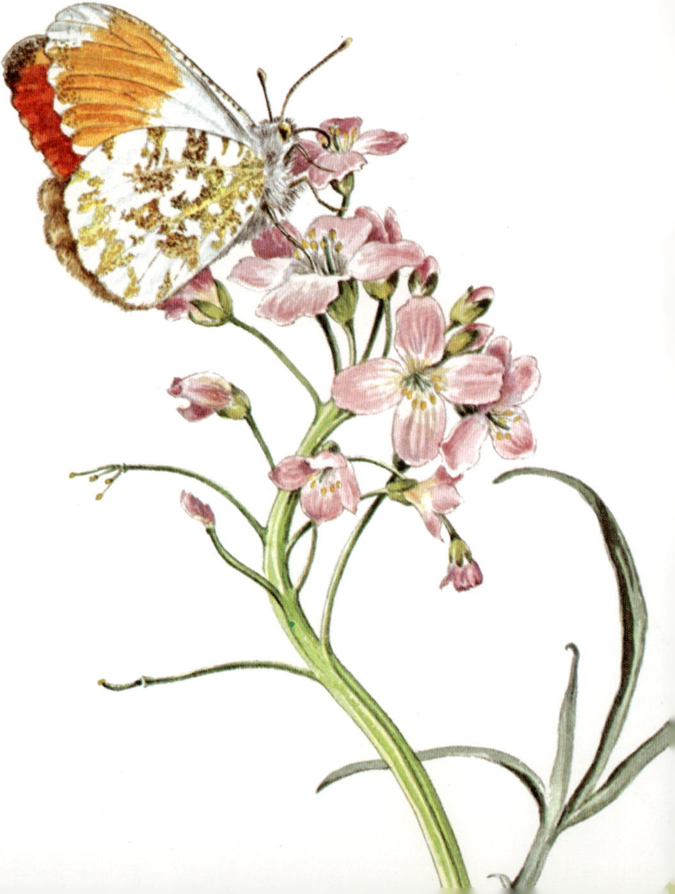

"Have you seen the honeybees?"
she asked an orange tip butterfly
sipping nectar from a cuckoo flower.
The butterfly was far too busy
to say anything at all.

"Have you seen the honeybees?" she asked three caterpillars munching on some nettle leaves. The caterpillars just kept munching.

"Have you seen the honeybees?"
she asked a scorpion fly
lazing on a rock-rose.
The fly wasn't listening.

"Oh, wherever can they be?"
wondered Busybee.
She watched some burnet moths
whirring lazily around
some knapweed flowers and,
suddenly, she felt very lonely.

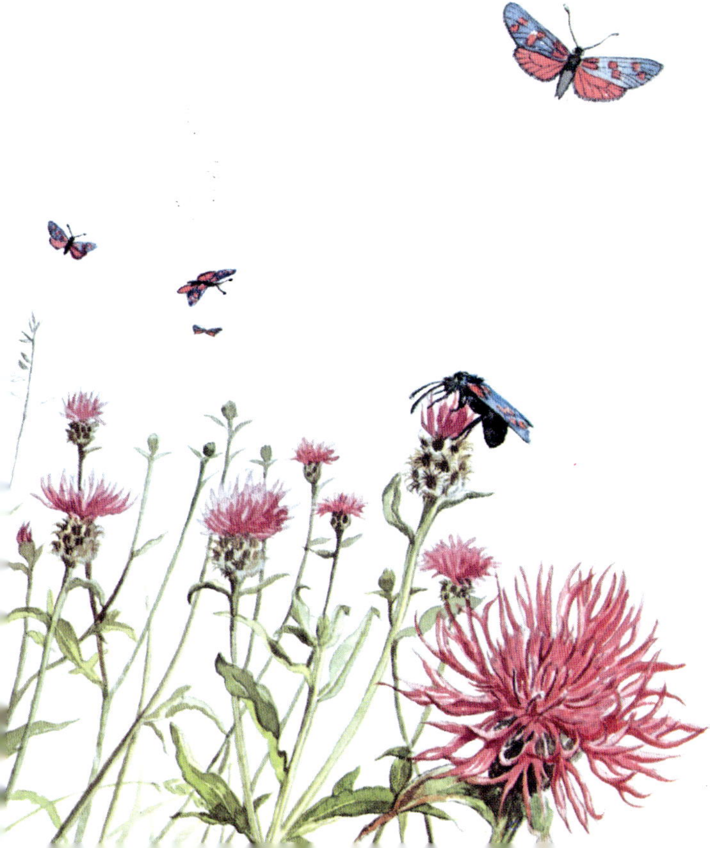

She headed towards the hedgerow
feeling rather sad.
There, on an enormous clump
of brambles, she spotted
all her friends, the honeybees.
"At last," she buzzed. "Hooray!"

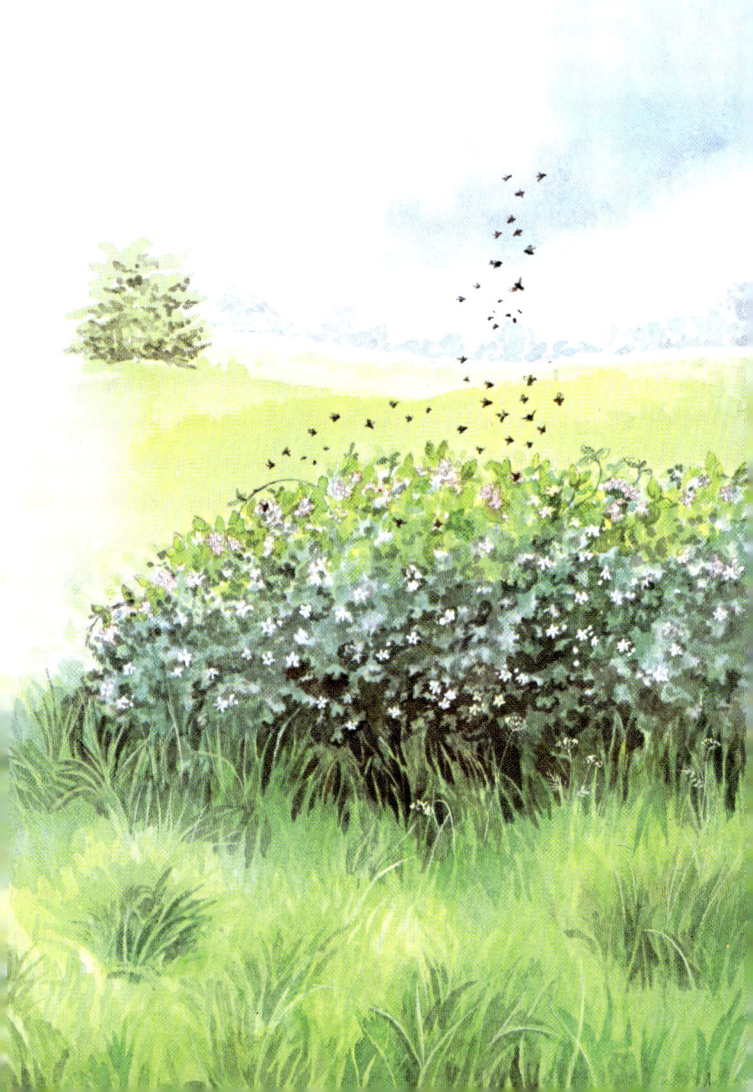

In her excitement, she didn't look where she was going.
Whoops!

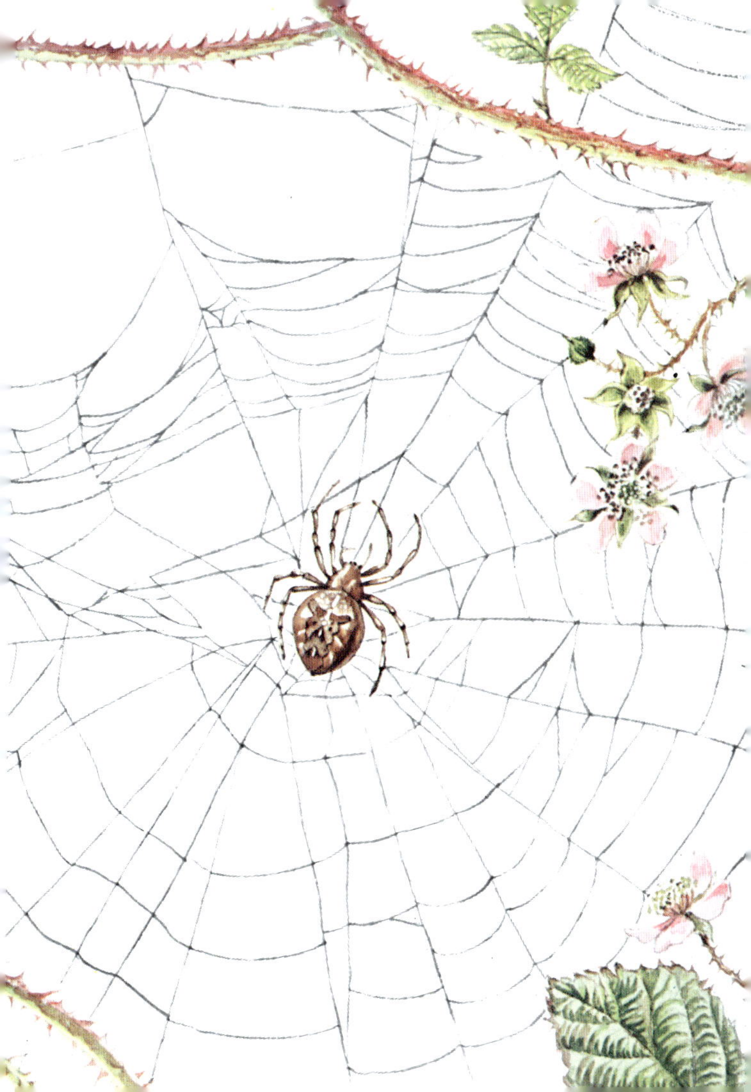

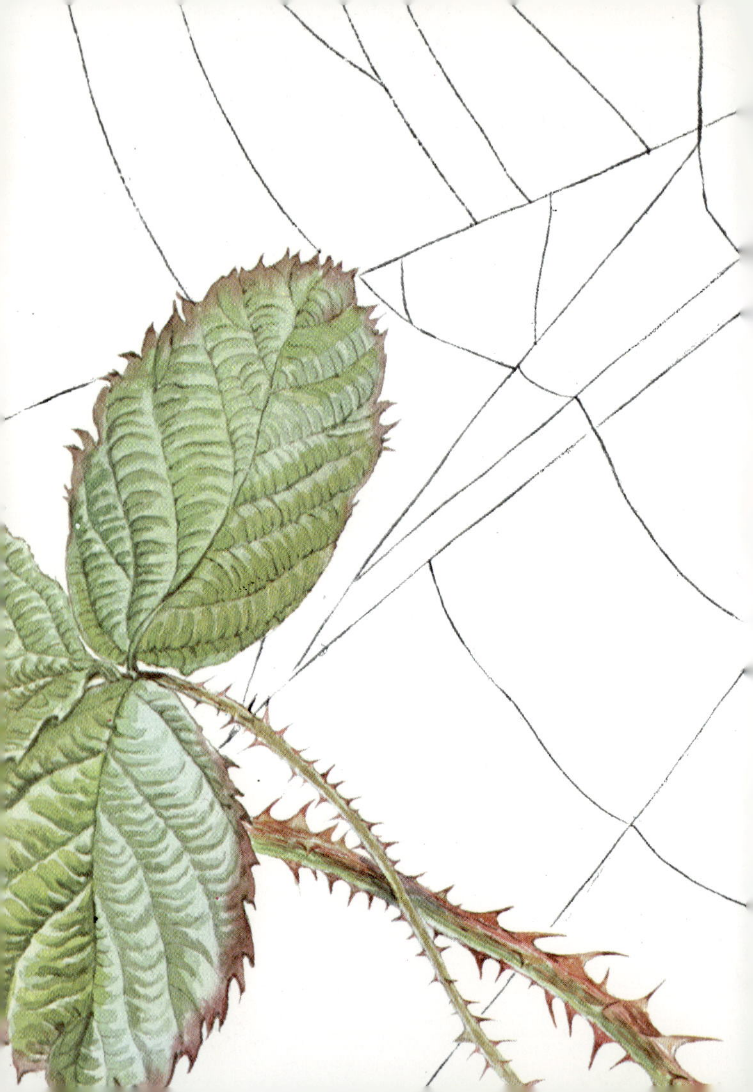

That was a near miss!
She almost flew into a spider's
web, cunningly hidden
in the brambles.

Bzz, bzz, bzz, bzz, bzz.
Busybee *was* glad to have found
her friends at last.
She sucked and sipped
as many flowers as she could
until it was time to leave.

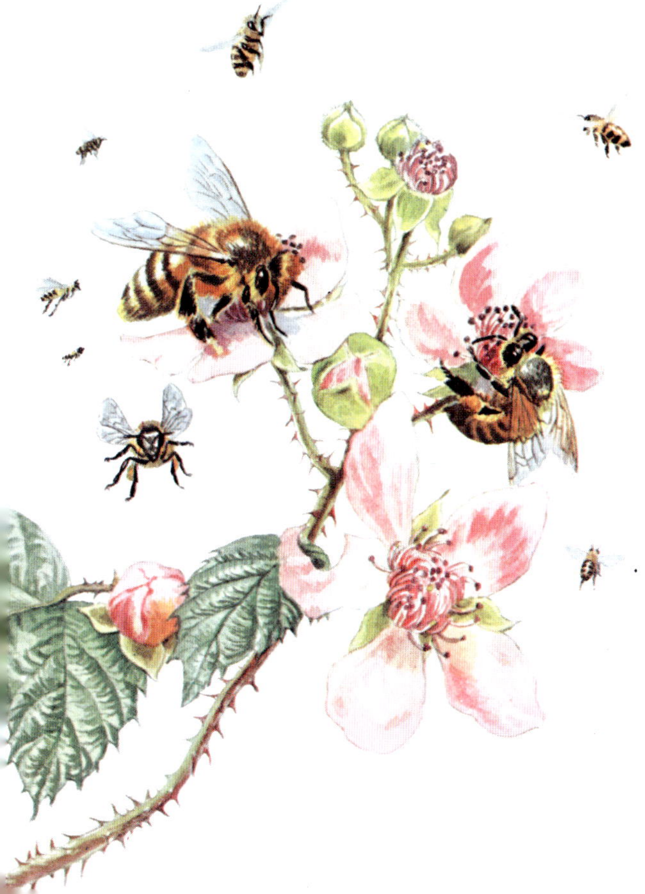

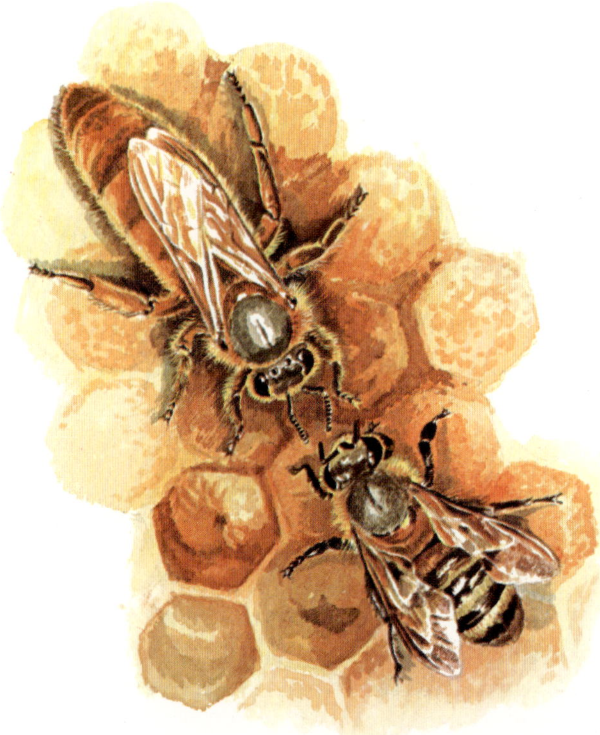

When Busybee got home
she told the queen
all about her busy day.
The queen smiled wisely and said,
"That will teach you
never to go out alone again."
And Busybee never did.

## MY NATURE LIBRARY

First Edition Copyright © 1982
The Reader's Digest Association
Limited, Berkeley Square House,
Berkeley Square, London W1X 6AB
Reprinted 1992

All rights reserved

® READER'S DIGEST, THE DIGEST and
the Pegasus logo are registered trademarks of
The Reader's Digest Association, Inc.
of Pleasantville, New York, U.S.A.

Phototypeset by Tradespools Limited
Frome, Somerset
Printed in Hong Kong
40.133.5